Minnie The Westie

The Adventures Of A
West Highland Terrier Cartoon Dog

by
Cornelia Luethi

FX Marketing Limited
Auckland, New Zealand

Minnie The Westie is online!

For more cartoons and Minnie's latest news, visit:

www.MinnieTheWestie.com

You can enjoy cartoons via email with Minnie Mail and connect with Minnie via social media.

National Library of New Zealand Cataloguing-in-Publication Data
Luethi, Cornelia, 1974-
Minnie the westie : the adventures of a west highland terrier cartoon dog / by Cornelia Luethi.
ISBN 978-0-473-19504-5
1. West Highland white terrier—Caricatures and cartoons.
2. West Highland white terrier—Humor. 3. New Zealand wit and humor, Pictorial. I. Title.
741.5993—dc 22

Published by FX Marketing Limited
Auckland, New Zealand

Version 1.0

"Nobody can fully understand the meaning of love unless he's owned a dog."

- Gene Hill

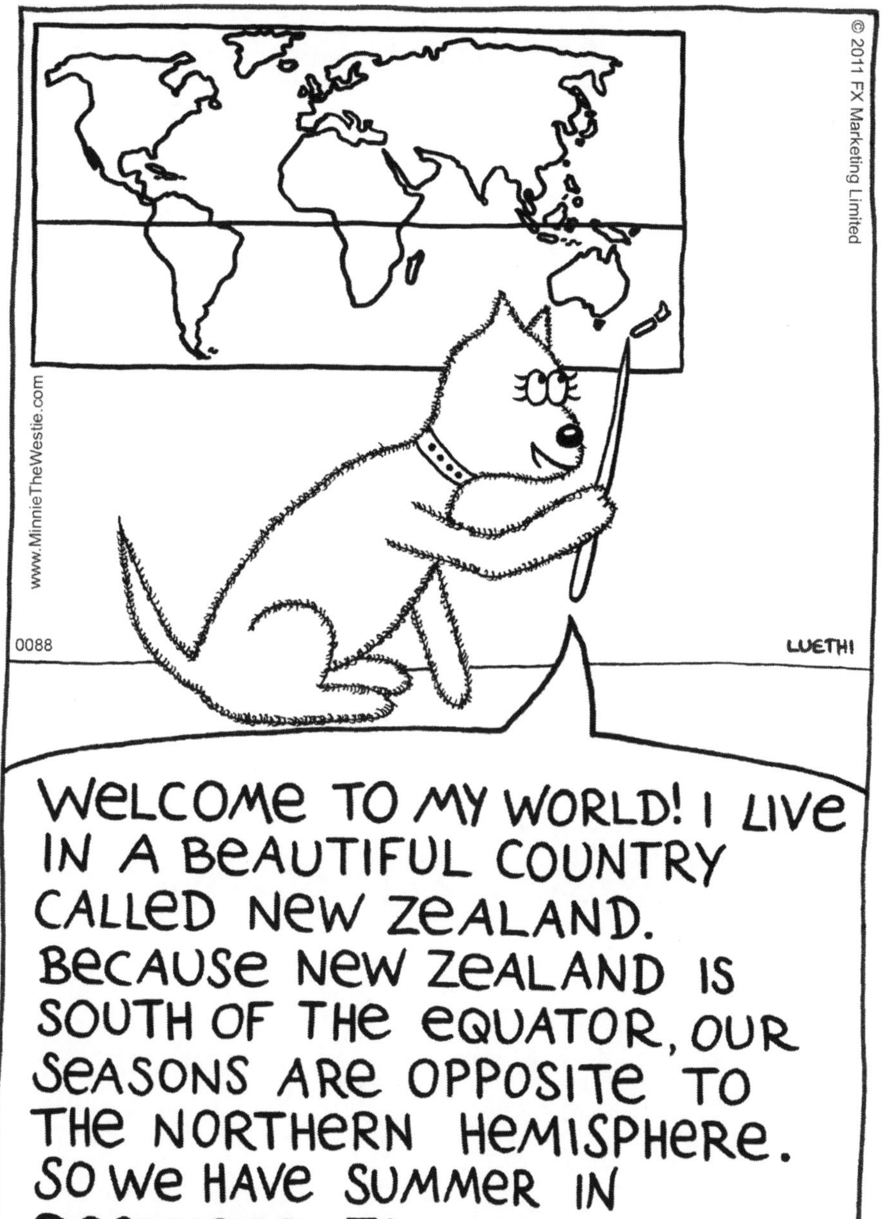
© 2011 FX Marketing Limited
www.MinnieTheWestie.com
0088
LUETHI
WELCOME TO MY WORLD! I LIVE IN A BEAUTIFUL COUNTRY CALLED NEW ZEALAND. BECAUSE NEW ZEALAND IS SOUTH OF THE EQUATOR, OUR SEASONS ARE OPPOSITE TO THE NORTHERN HEMISPHERE. SO WE HAVE SUMMER IN DECEMBER, JANUARY AND FEBRUARY, WHILE JUNE, JULY AND AUGUST ARE WINTER.

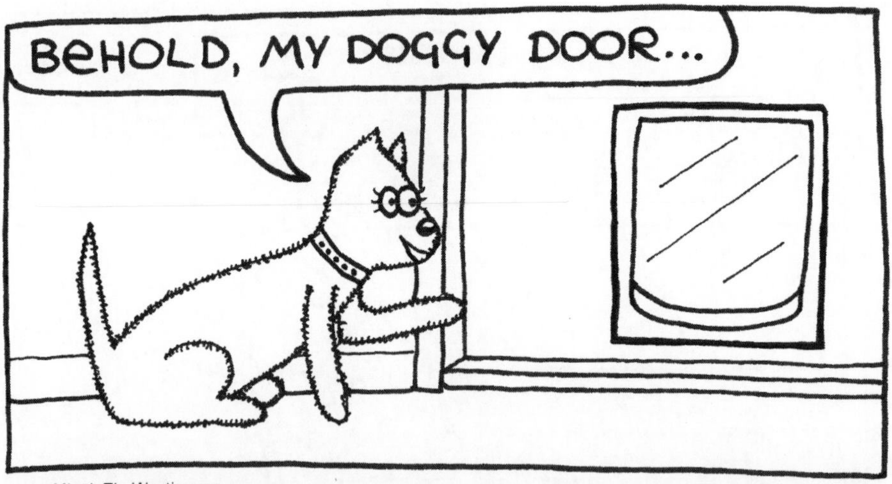
BEHOLD, MY DOGGY DOOR...

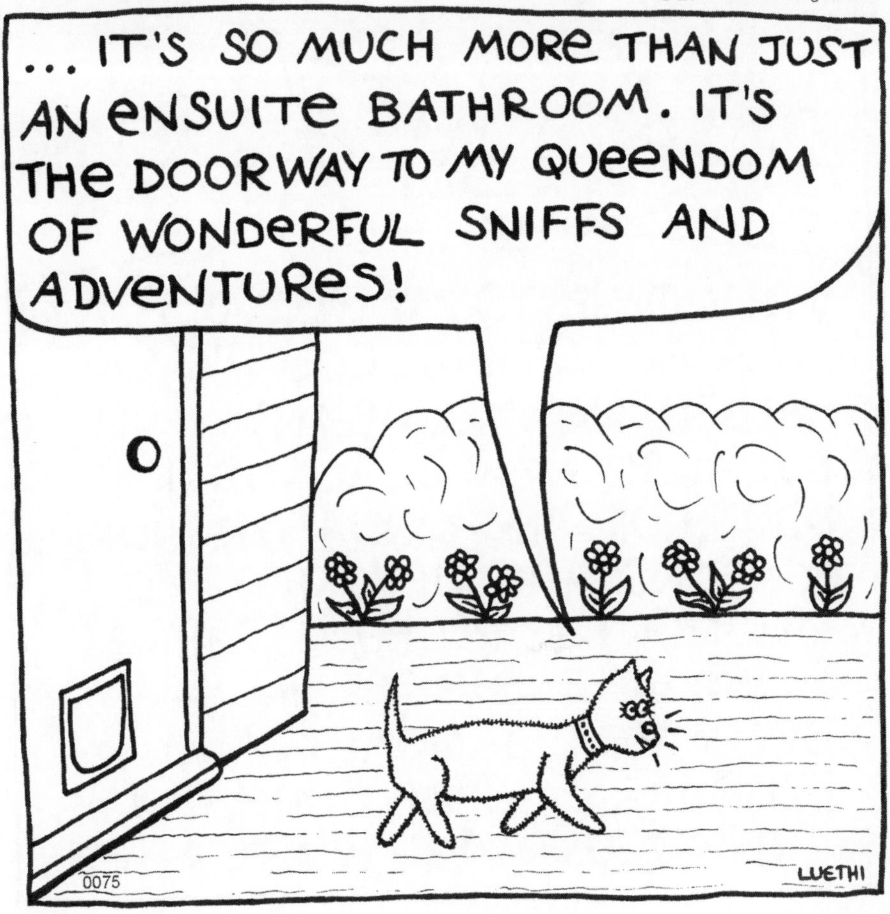
... IT'S SO MUCH MORE THAN JUST AN ENSUITE BATHROOM. IT'S THE DOORWAY TO MY QUEENDOM OF WONDERFUL SNIFFS AND ADVENTURES!
0075
LUETHI

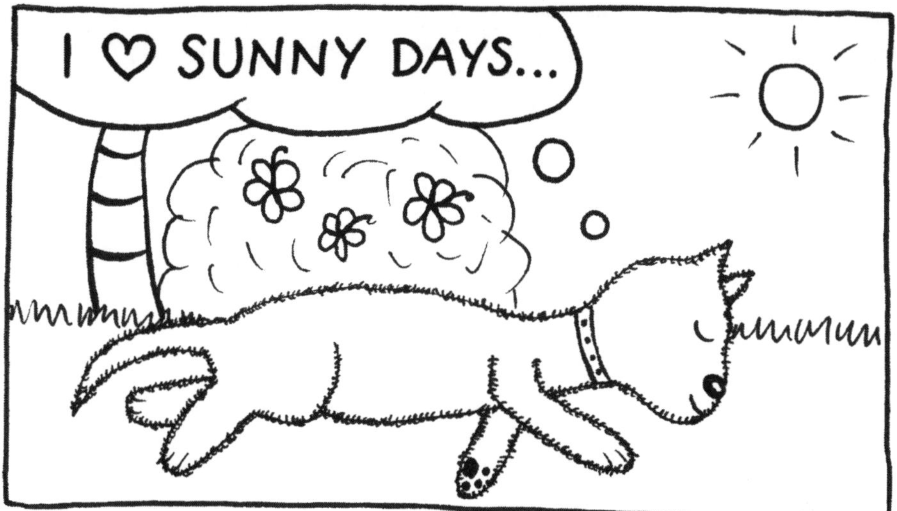
I ♡ SUNNY DAYS...

www.MinnieTheWestie.com

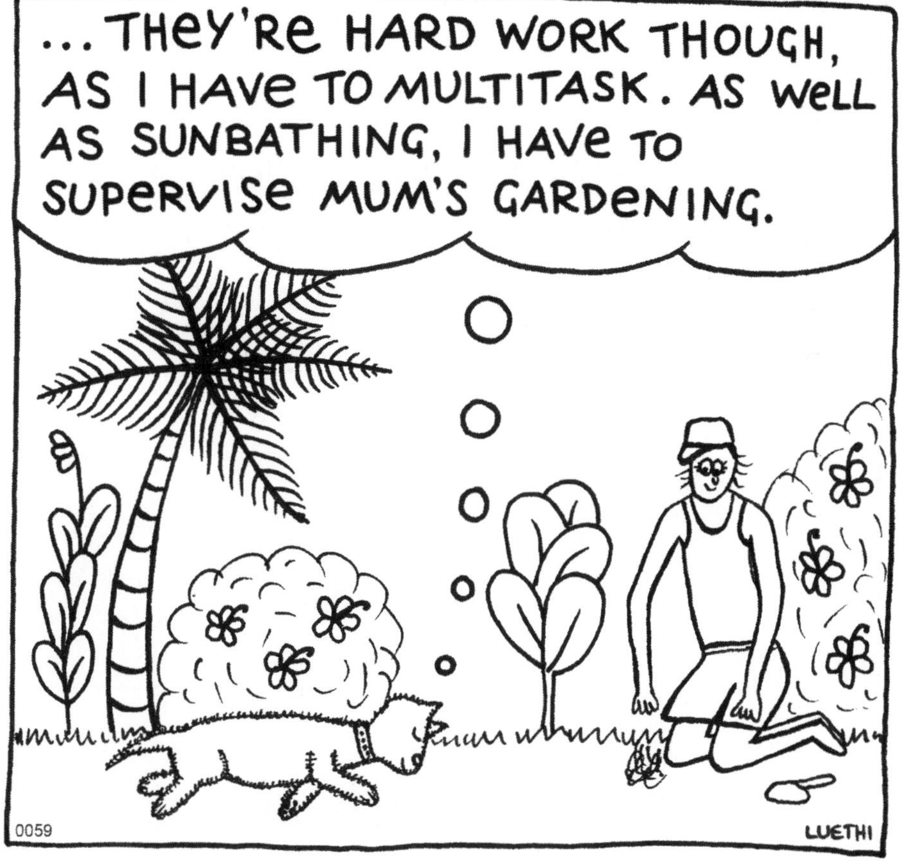
...THEY'RE HARD WORK THOUGH, AS I HAVE TO MULTITASK. AS WELL AS SUNBATHING, I HAVE TO SUPERVISE MUM'S GARDENING.
0059
LUETHI

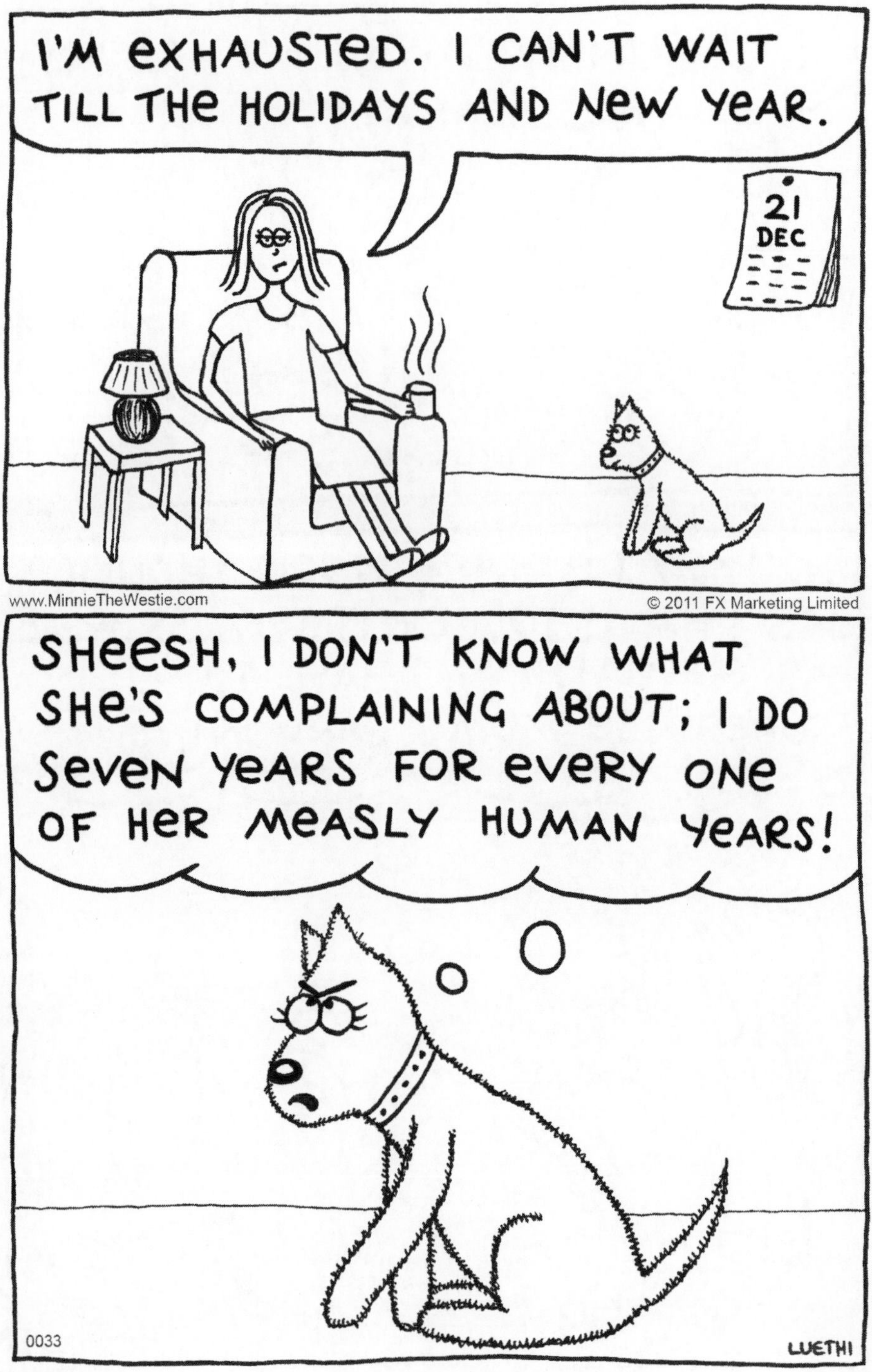

I'M EXHAUSTED. I CAN'T WAIT TILL THE HOLIDAYS AND NEW YEAR.
21 DEC
www.MinnieTheWestie.com
© 2011 FX Marketing Limited
SHEESH, I DON'T KNOW WHAT SHE'S COMPLAINING ABOUT; I DO SEVEN YEARS FOR EVERY ONE OF HER MEASLY HUMAN YEARS!
0033
LUETHI

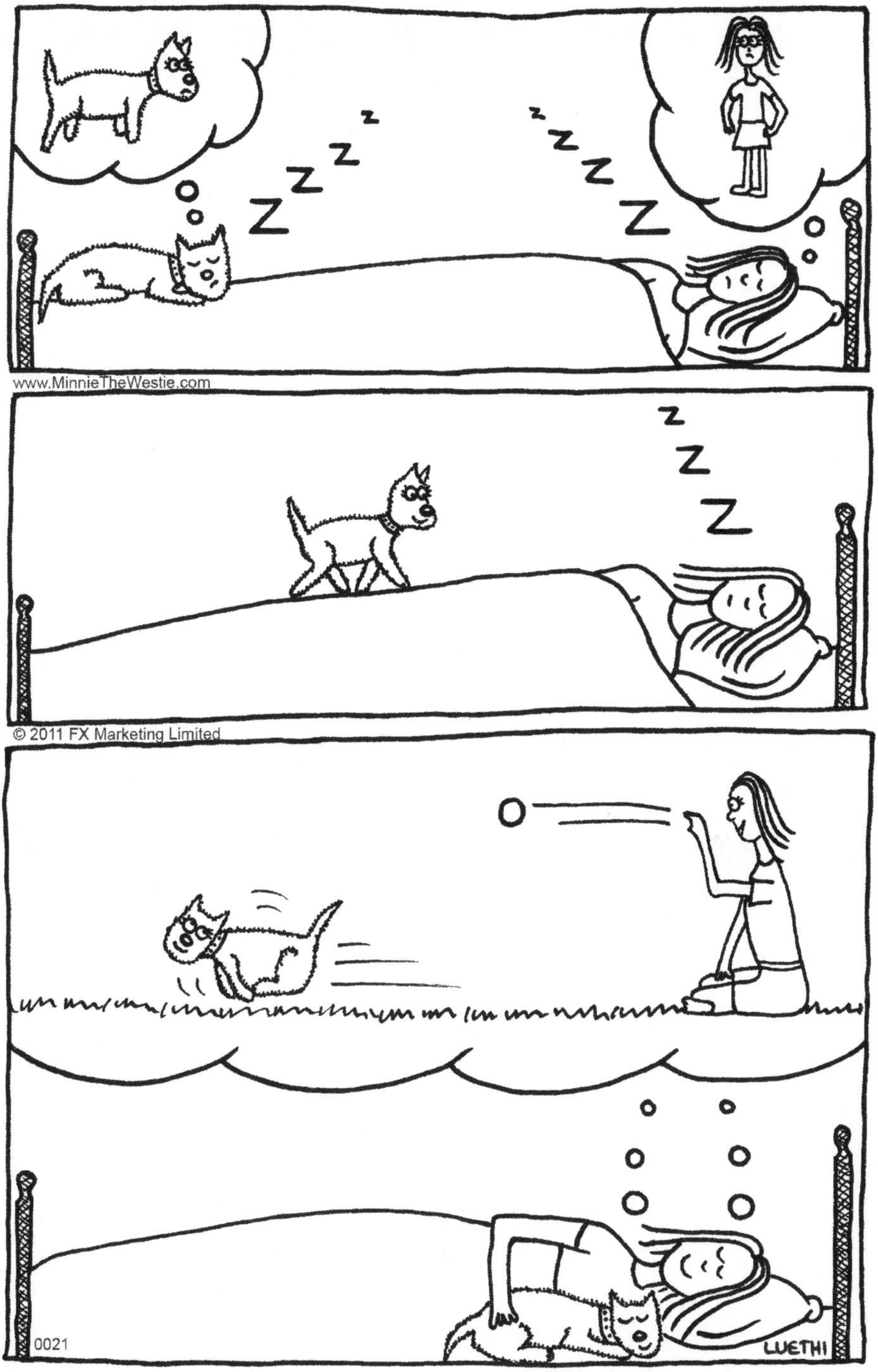

Z Z Z Z
Z Z Z Z
www.MinnieTheWestie.com
Z Z Z
© 2011 FX Marketing Limited
0021
LUETHI

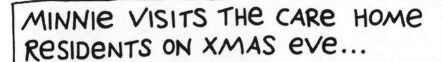

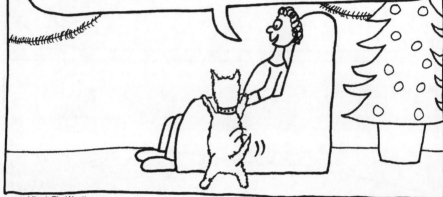

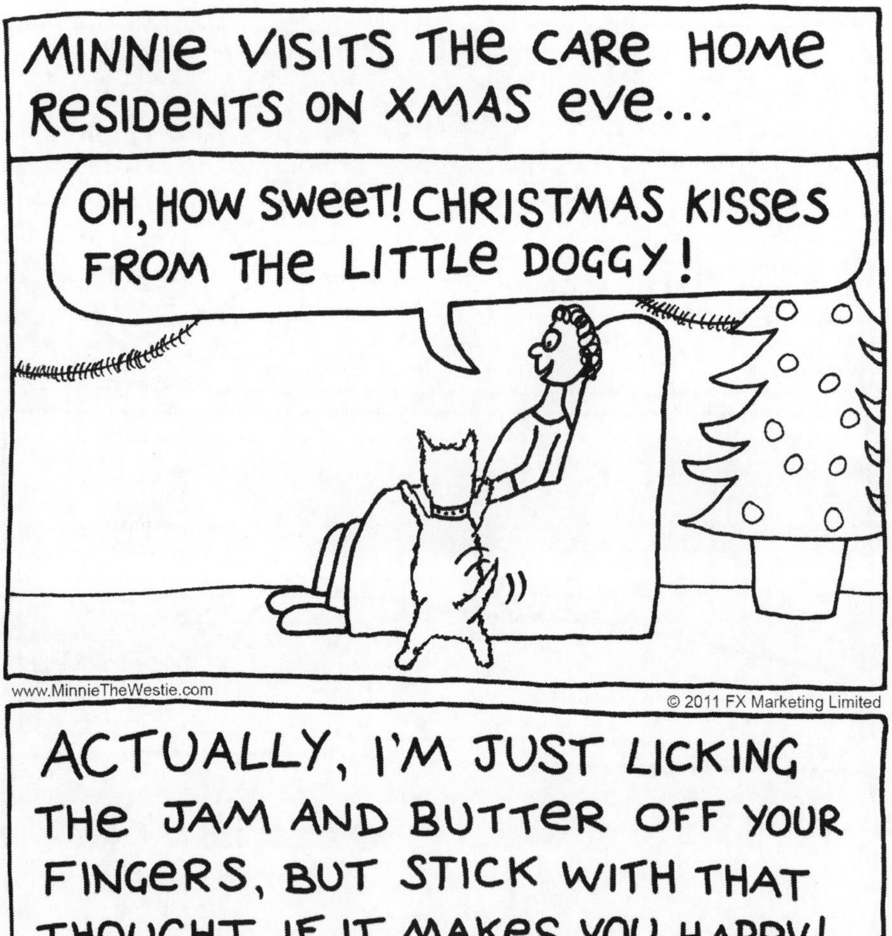

MINNIE VISITS THE CARE HOME RESIDENTS ON XMAS EVE...
OH, HOW SWEET! CHRISTMAS KISSES FROM THE LITTLE DOGGY!
www.MinnieTheWestie.com
© 2011 FX Marketing Limited
ACTUALLY, I'M JUST LICKING THE JAM AND BUTTER OFF YOUR FINGERS, BUT STICK WITH THAT THOUGHT IF IT MAKES YOU HAPPY!
0002
LUETHI

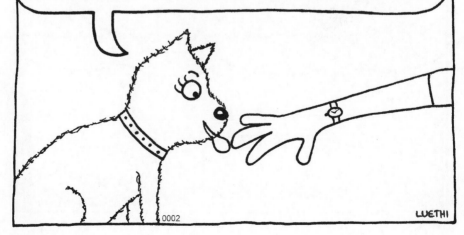

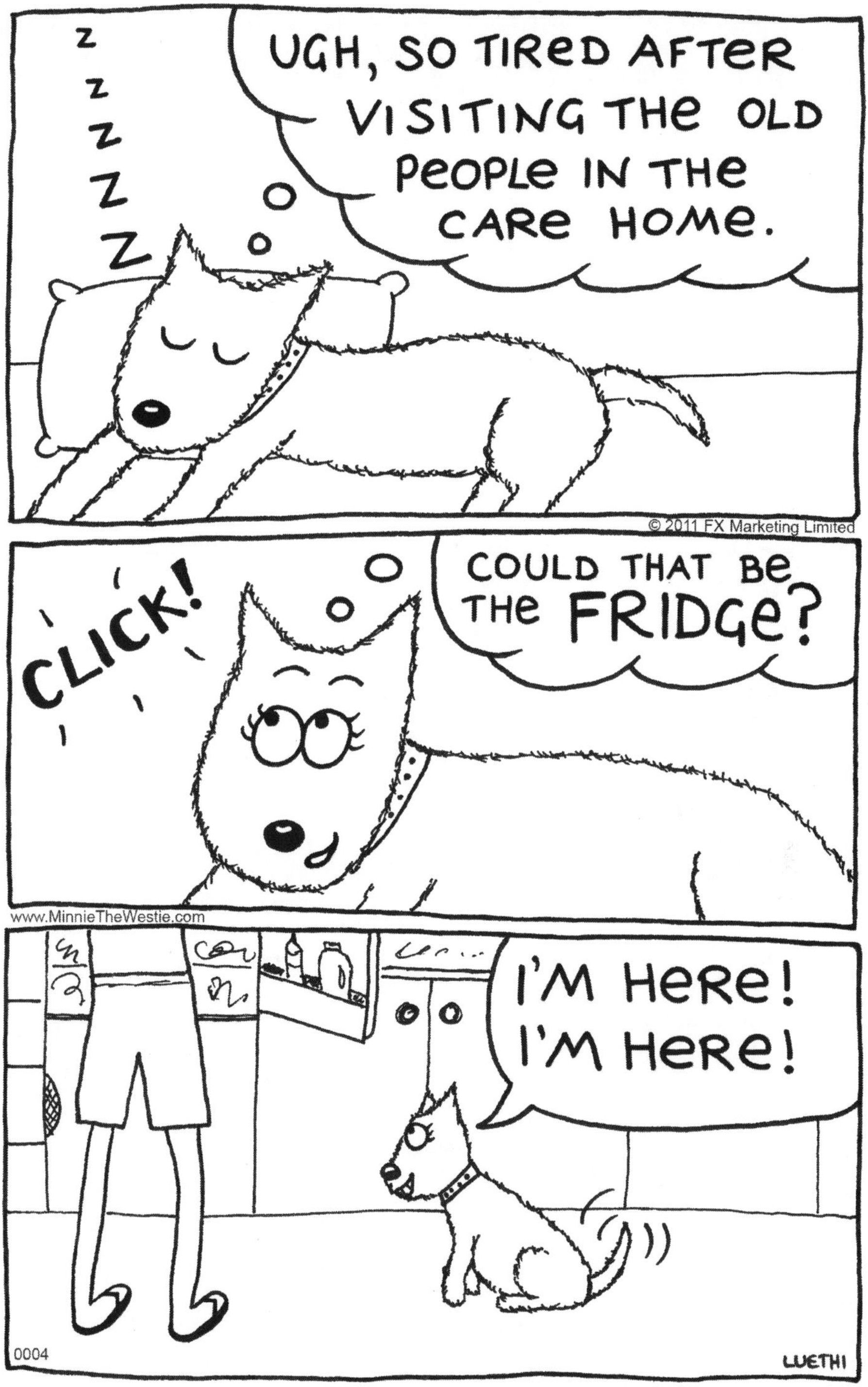
Z Z Z Z Z
UGH, SO TIRED AFTER VISITING THE OLD PEOPLE IN THE CARE HOME.
© 2011 FX Marketing Limited
CLICK!
COULD THAT BE THE FRIDGE?
www.MinnieTheWestie.com
I'M HERE! I'M HERE!
0004
LUETHI

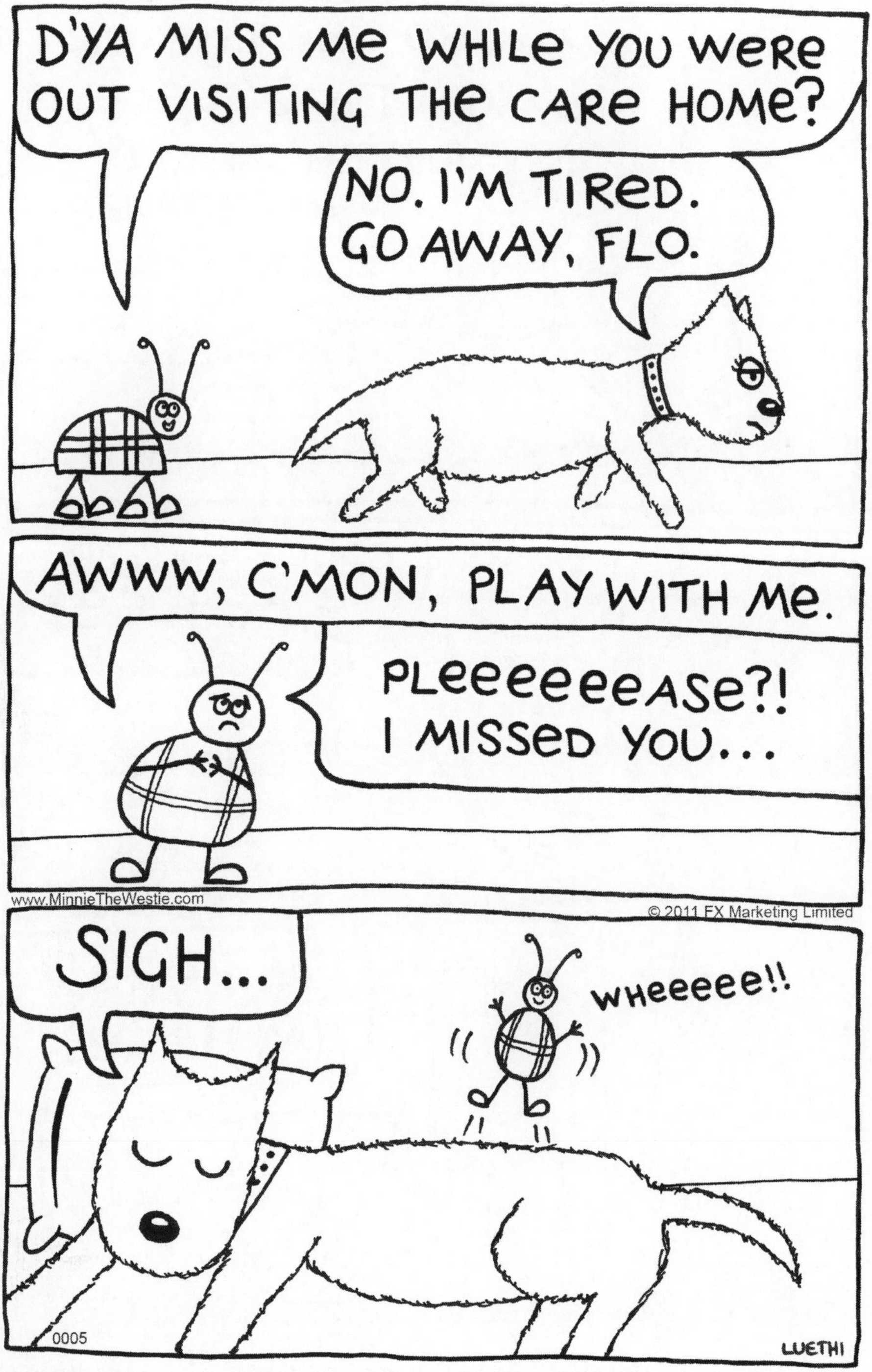
D'YA MISS ME WHILE YOU WERE OUT VISITING THE CARE HOME?
NO. I'M TIRED. GO AWAY, FLO.
AWWW, C'MON, PLAY WITH ME.
PLEEEEEEEASE?! I MISSED YOU...
www.MinnieTheWestie.com
© 2011 FX Marketing Limited
SIGH...
WHEEEEE!!
0005
LUETHI

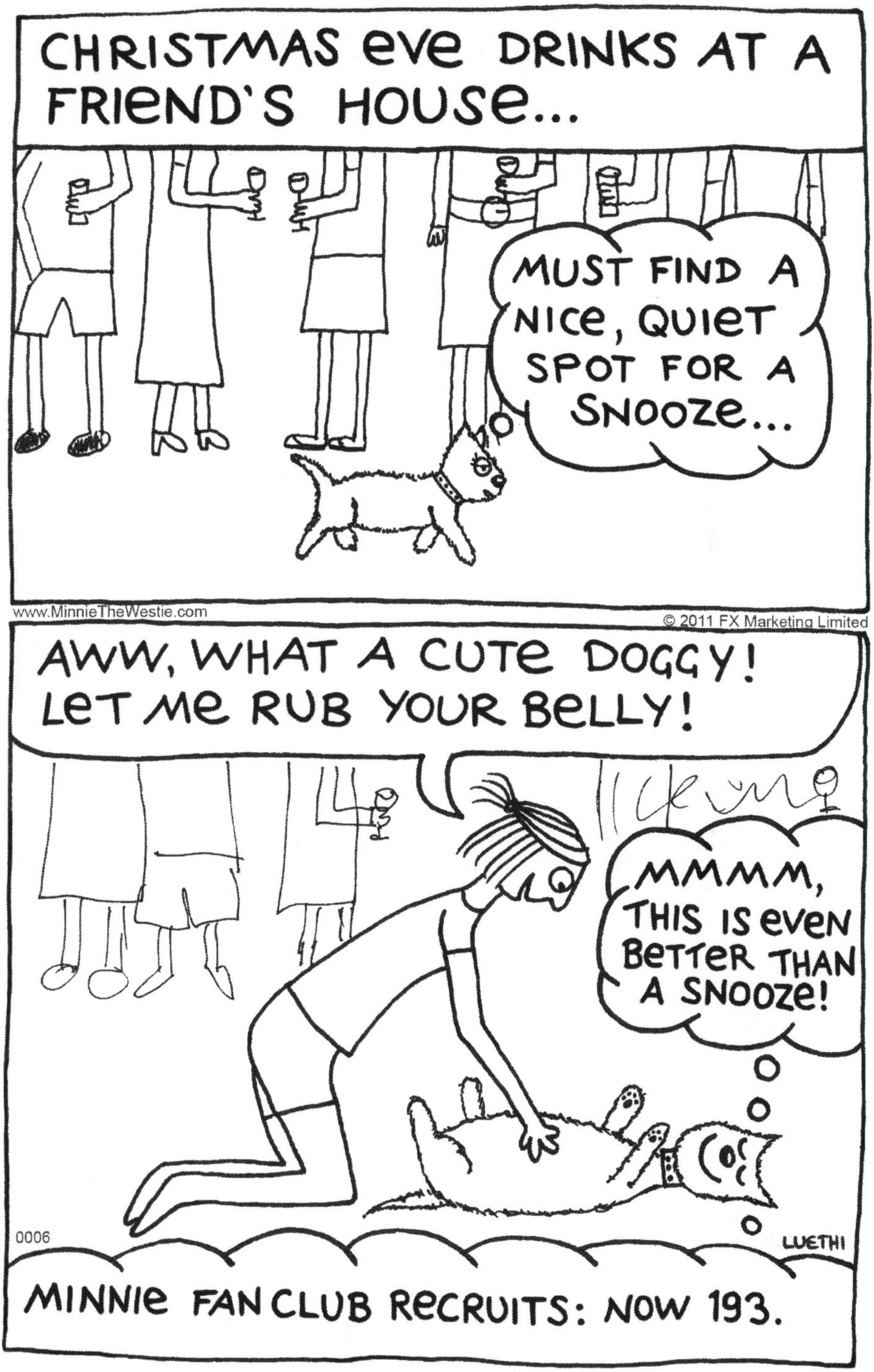
CHRISTMAS eve DRINKS AT A FRIEND'S HOUSE...
MUST FIND A NICE, QUIET SPOT FOR A SNOOZE...
www.MinnieTheWestie.com
© 2011 FX Marketing Limited
AWW, WHAT A CUTE DOGGY! LET ME RUB YOUR BELLY!
MMMM, THIS IS even BETTER THAN A SNOOZE!
0006
LUETHI
MINNIe FAN CLUB ReCRUITS: NOW 193.

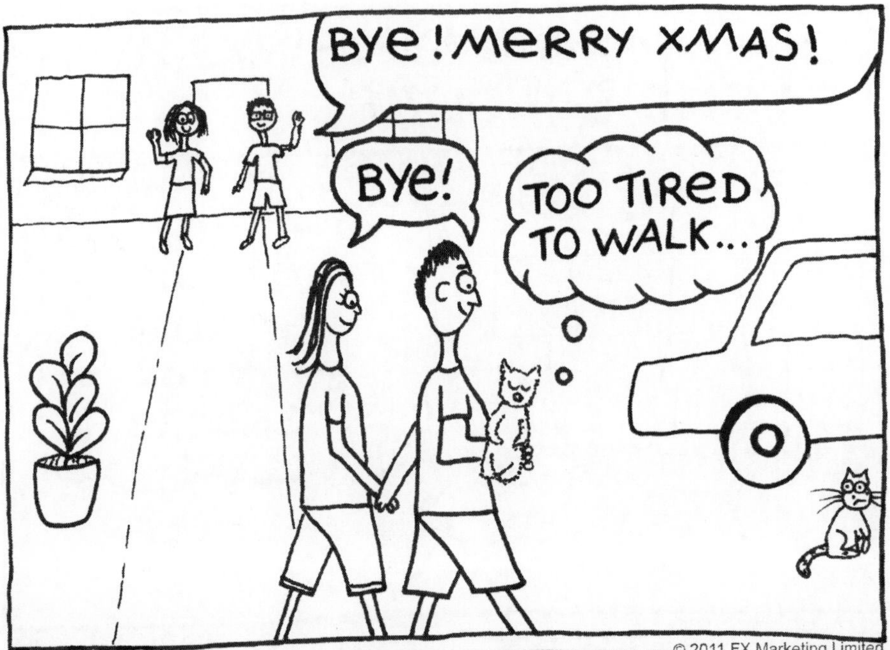
BYE! MERRY XMAS!
BYE!
TOO TIRED TO WALK...

www.MinnieTheWestie.com

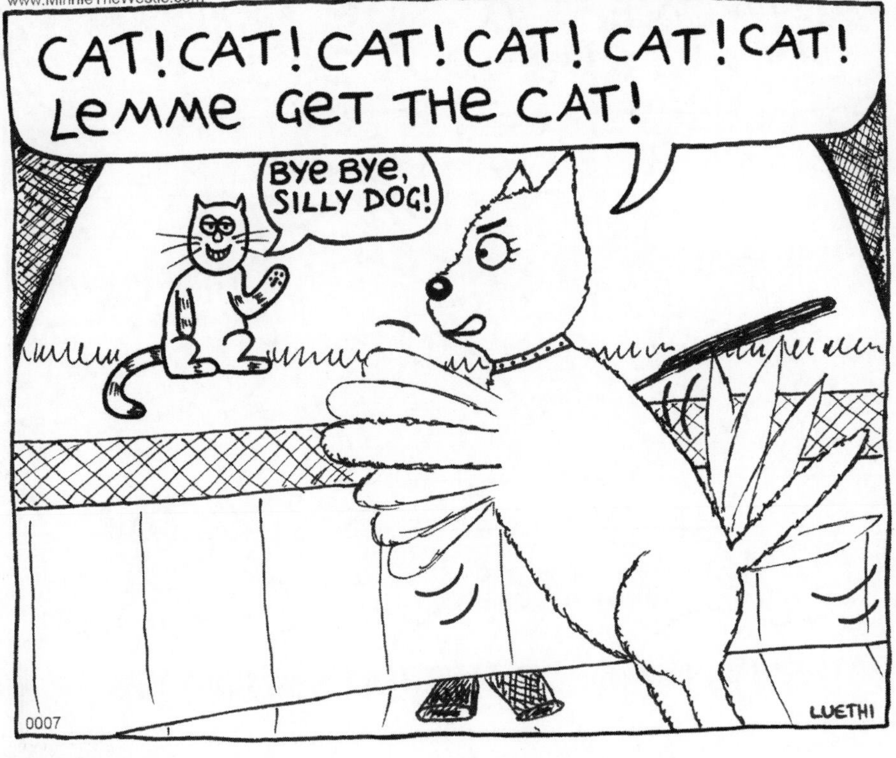
CAT! CAT! CAT! CAT! CAT! CAT!
LEMME GET THE CAT!
BYE BYE, SILLY DOG!
0007
LUETHI

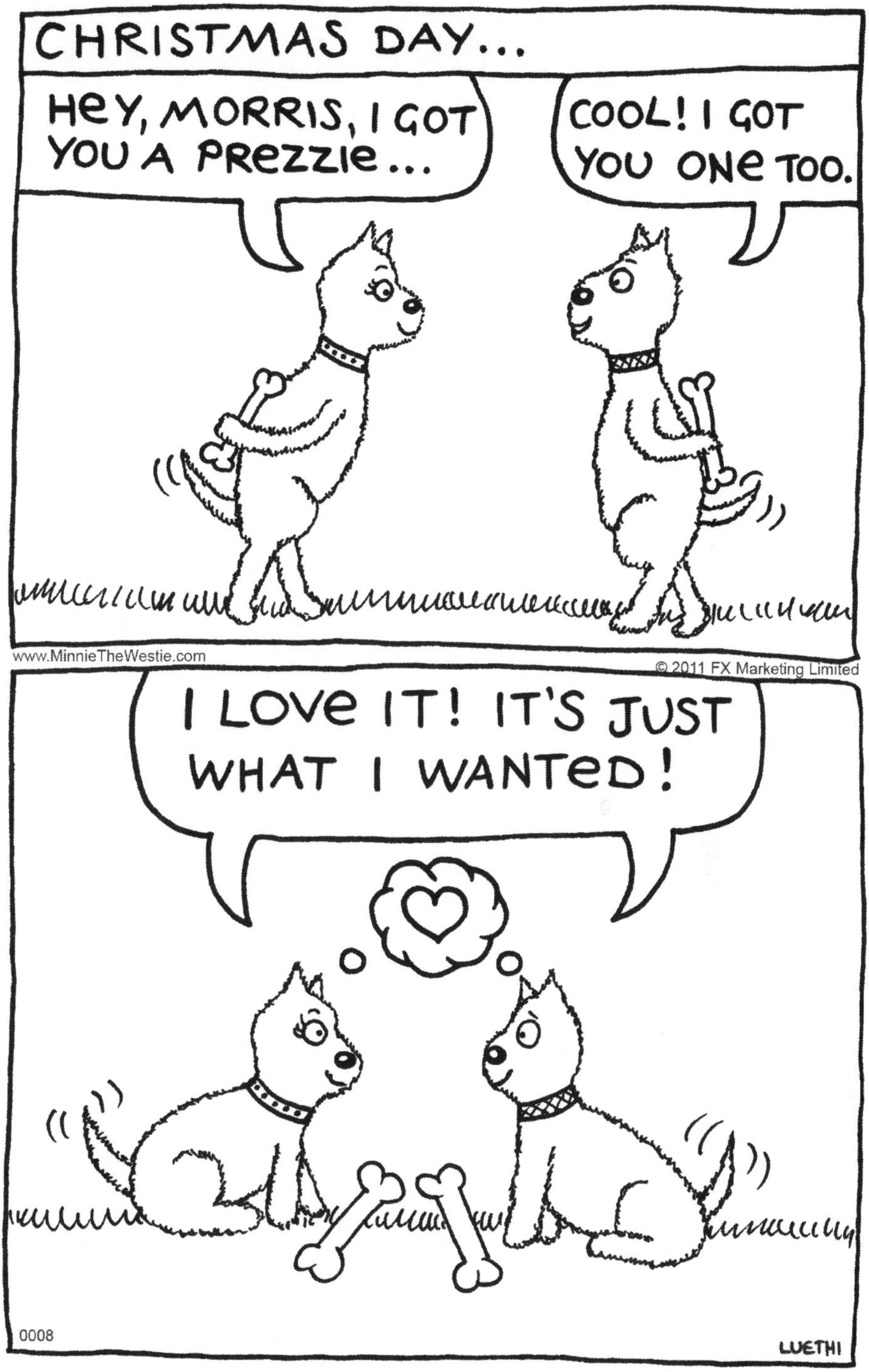
CHRISTMAS DAY...
HEY, MORRIS, I GOT YOU A PREZZIE...
COOL! I GOT YOU ONE TOO.
www.MinnieTheWestie.com
© 2011 FX Marketing Limited
I LOVE IT! IT'S JUST WHAT I WANTED!
0008
LUETHI

MERRY CHRISTMAS, MINNIE!
www.MinnieTheWestie.com
© 2011 FX Marketing Limited
I HAVE NO IDEA WHAT THIS 'CHRISTMAS' IS THAT YOU SPEAK OF, BUT I'LL NEVER SAY NO TO A NEW TOY!
SQUEAK!
SQUEAK!
0009
LUETHI

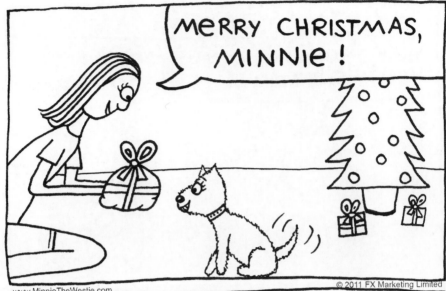

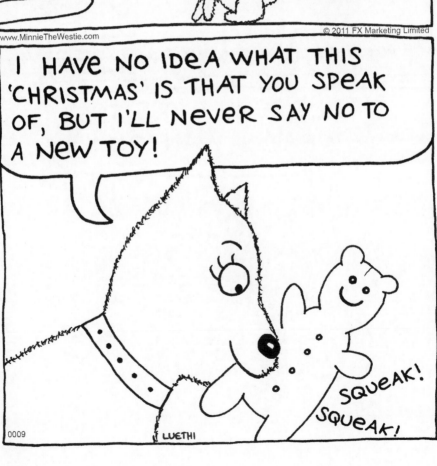

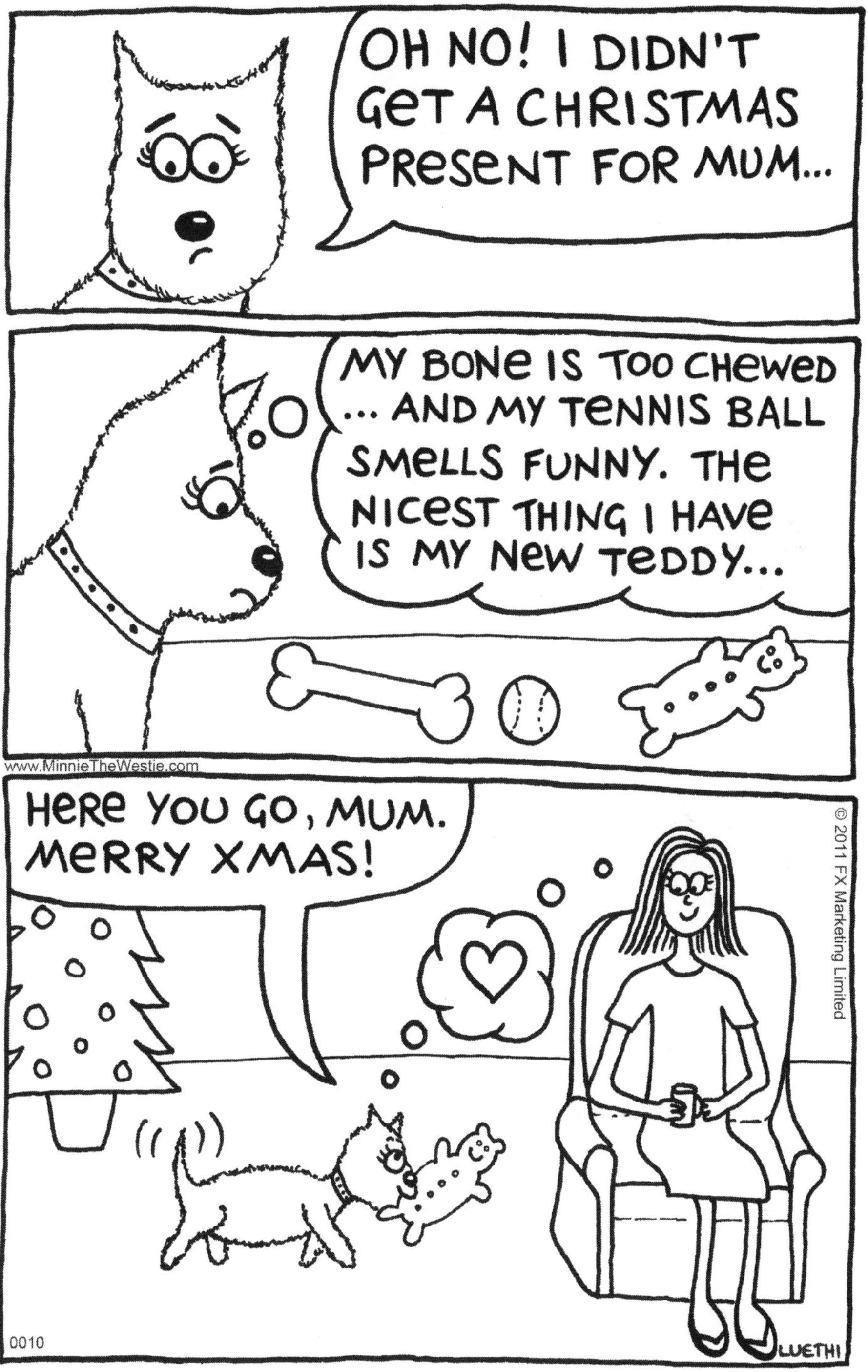

OH NO! I DIDN'T GET A CHRISTMAS PRESENT FOR MUM...
MY BONE IS TOO CHEWED ... AND MY TENNIS BALL SMELLS FUNNY. THE NICEST THING I HAVE IS MY NEW TEDDY...
www.MinnieTheWestie.com
HERE YOU GO, MUM. MERRY XMAS!
© 2011 FX Marketing Limited
0010
LUETHI

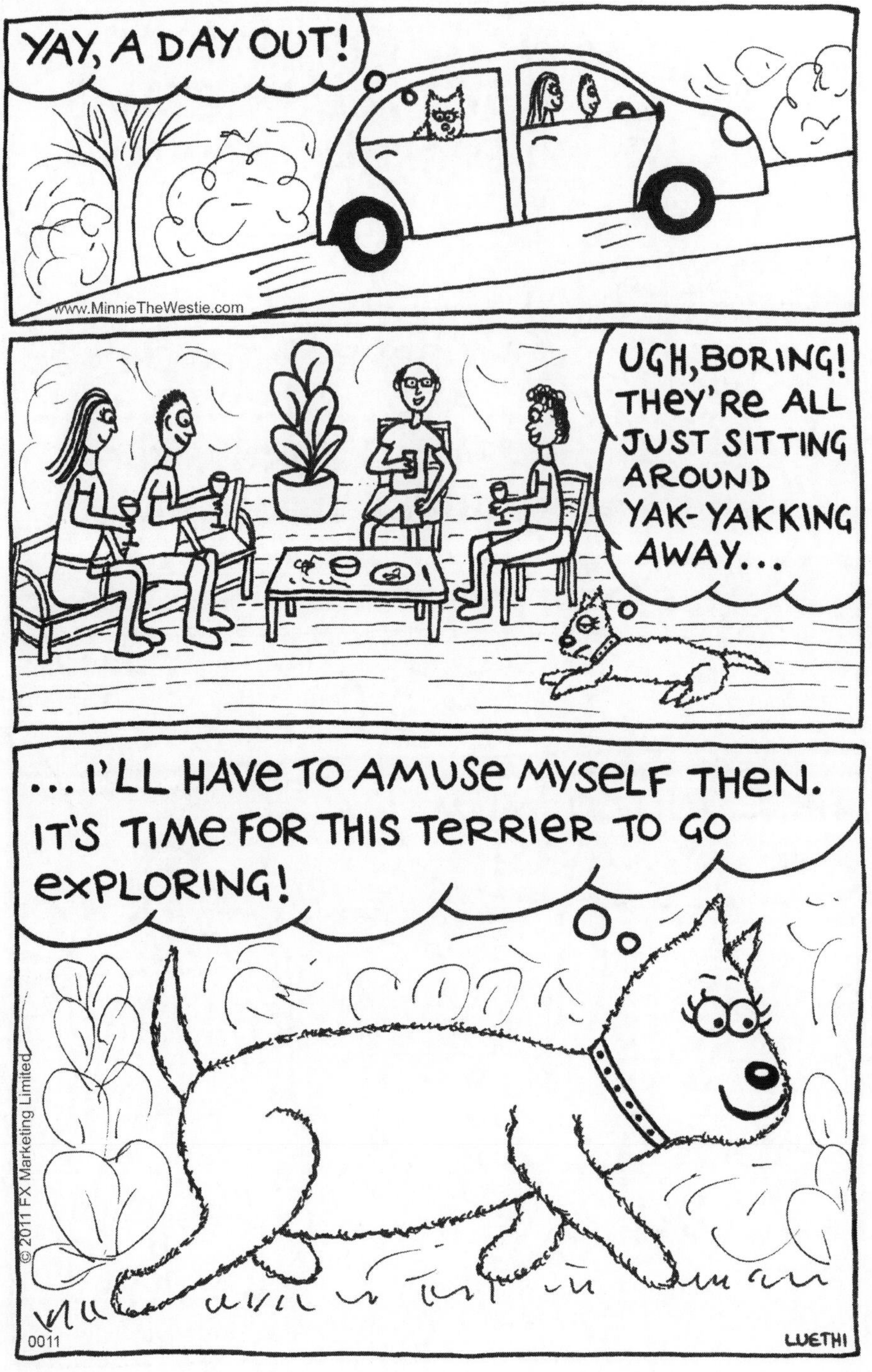
YAY, A DAY OUT!
www.MinnieTheWestie.com
UGH, BORING! THEY'RE ALL JUST SITTING AROUND YAK-YAKKING AWAY...
...I'LL HAVE TO AMUSE MYSELF THEN. IT'S TIME FOR THIS TERRIER TO GO EXPLORING!
© 2011 FX Marketing Limited
0011
LUETHI

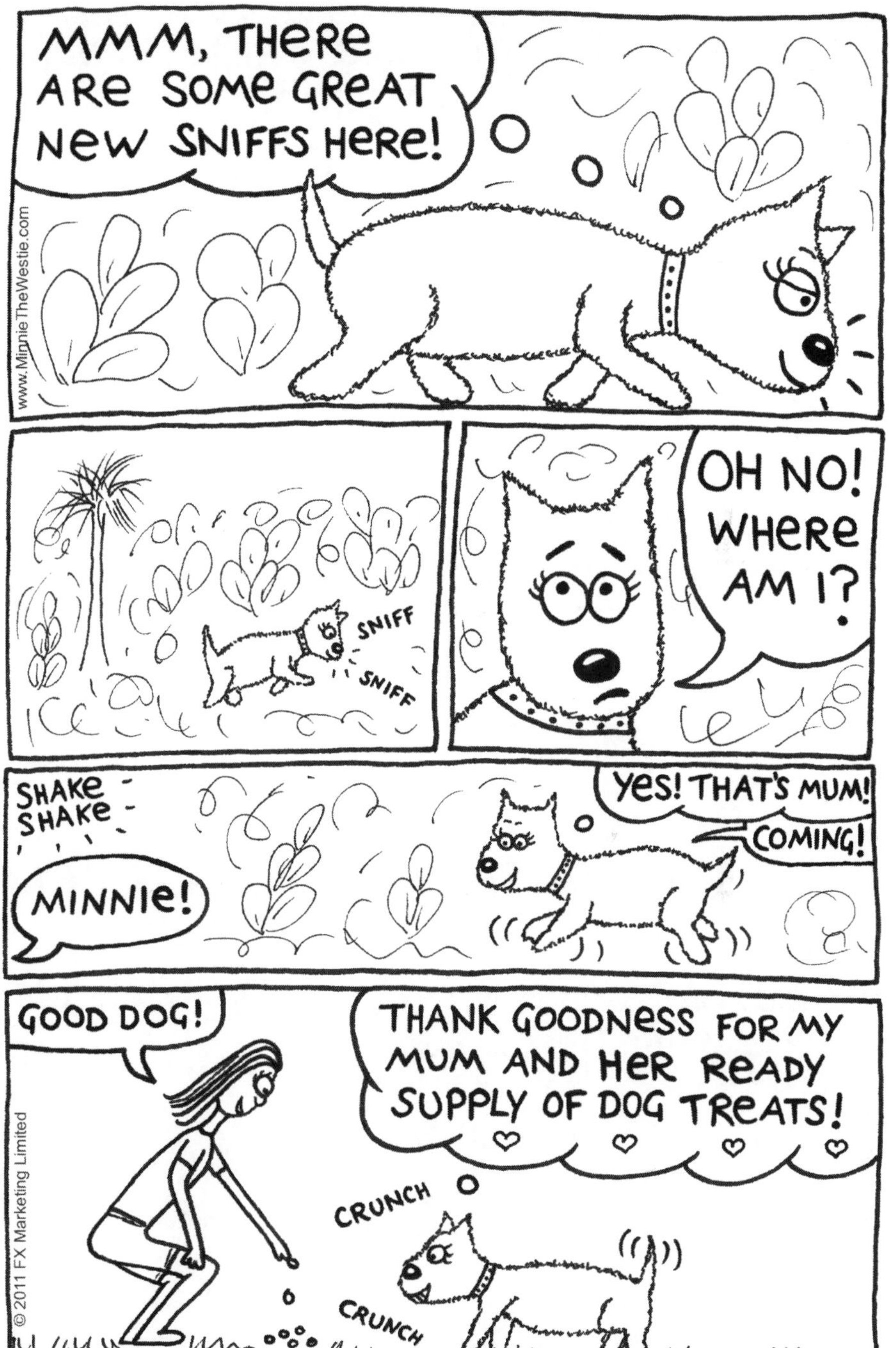
MMM, THERE ARE SOME GREAT NEW SNIFFS HERE!
www.MinnieTheWestie.com
SNIFF
SNIFF
OH NO! WHERE AM I?
SHAKE SHAKE
MINNIE!
YES! THAT'S MUM!
COMING!
GOOD DOG!
THANK GOODNESS FOR MY MUM AND HER READY SUPPLY OF DOG TREATS!
CRUNCH
CRUNCH
© 2011 FX Marketing Limited
0012
LUETHI

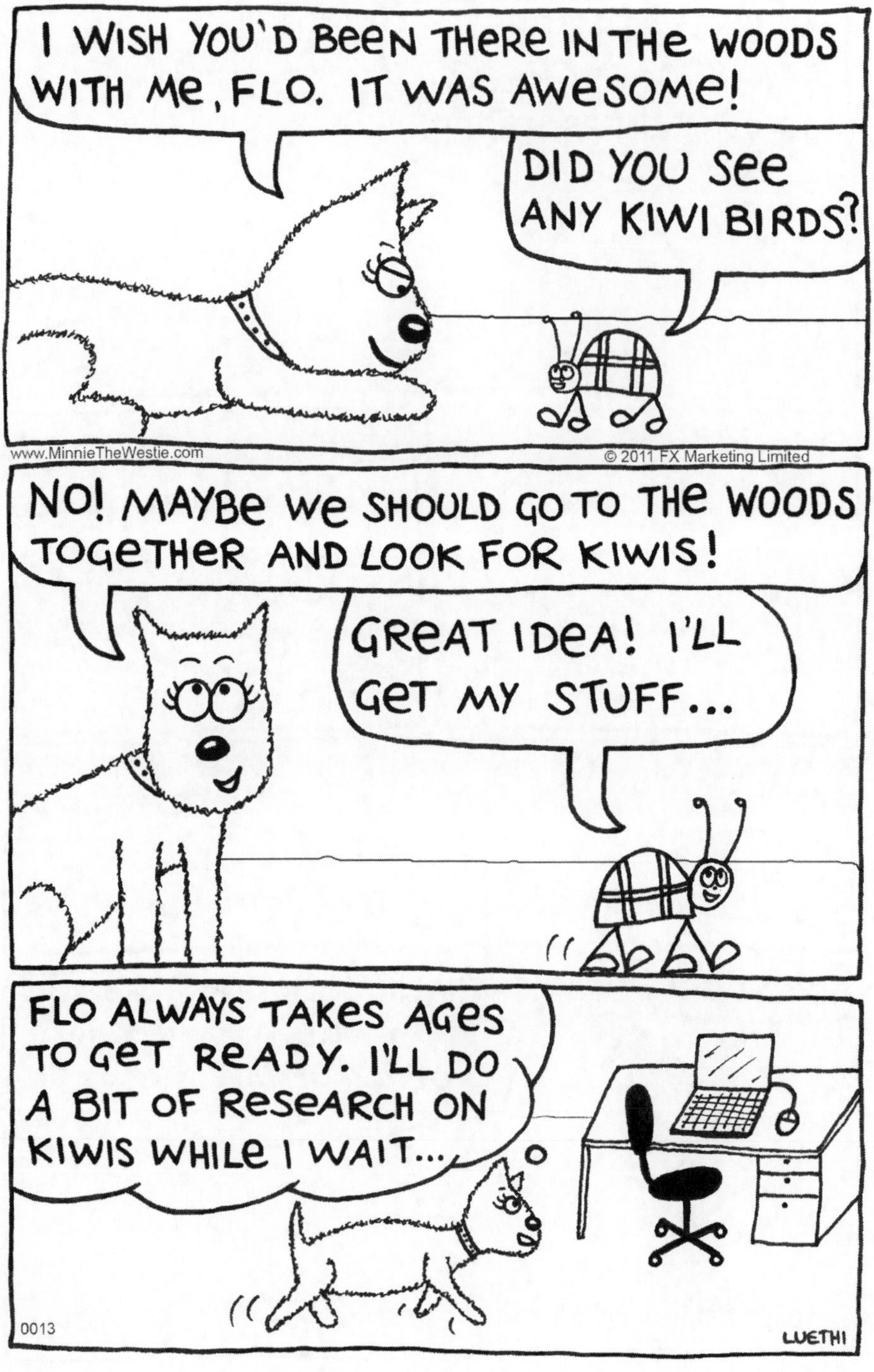
I WISH YOU'D BEEN THERE IN THE WOODS WITH ME, FLO. IT WAS AWESOME!
DID YOU SEE ANY KIWI BIRDS?
www.MinnieTheWestie.com
© 2011 FX Marketing Limited
NO! MAYBE WE SHOULD GO TO THE WOODS TOGETHER AND LOOK FOR KIWIS!
GREAT IDEA! I'LL GET MY STUFF...
FLO ALWAYS TAKES AGES TO GET READY. I'LL DO A BIT OF RESEARCH ON KIWIS WHILE I WAIT...
0013
LUETHI

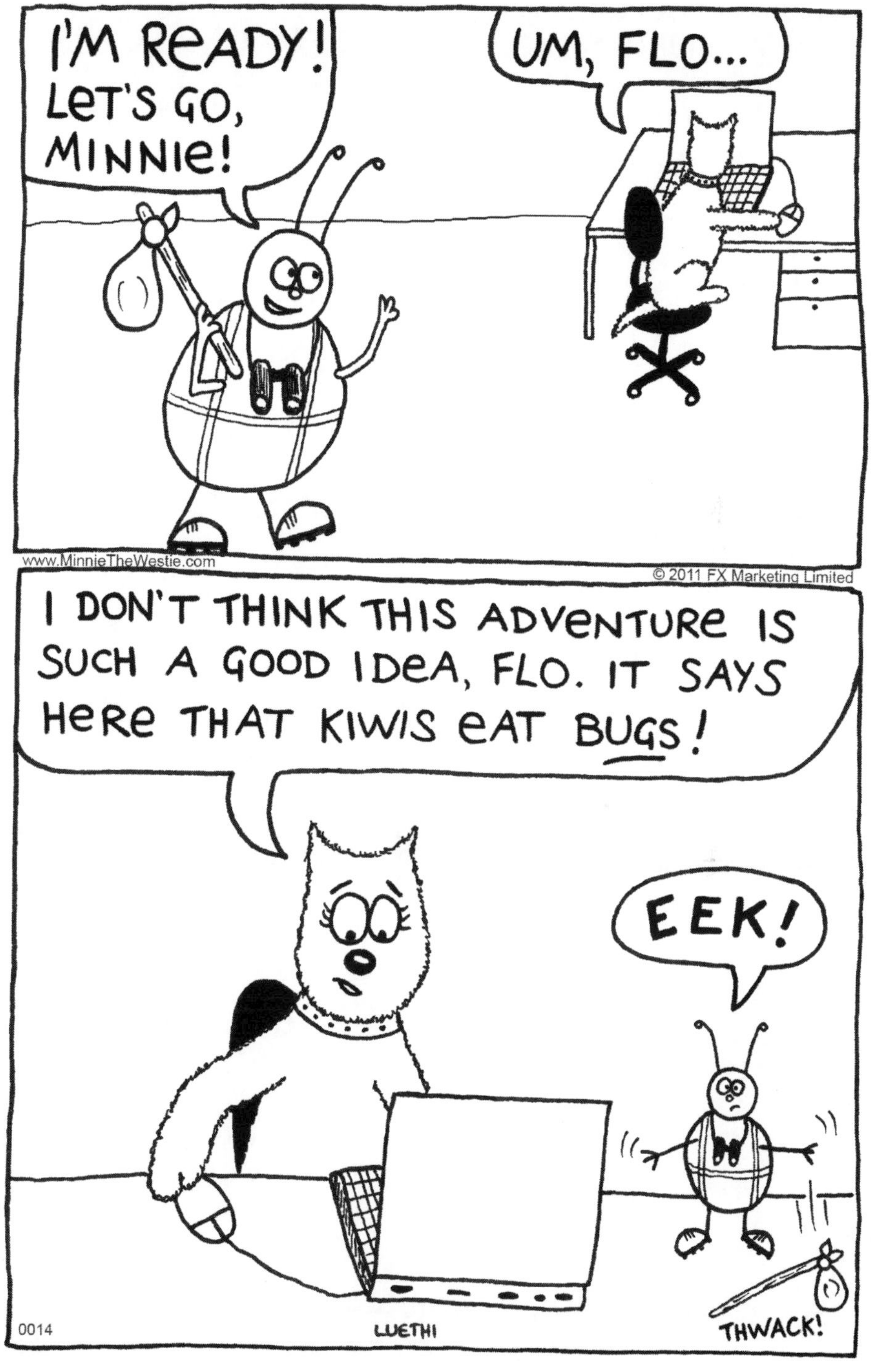
I'M READY! LET'S GO, MINNIE!
UM, FLO...
www.MinnieTheWestie.com
© 2011 FX Marketing Limited
I DON'T THINK THIS ADVENTURE IS SUCH A GOOD IDEA, FLO. IT SAYS HERE THAT KIWIS EAT BUGS!
EEK!
0014
LUETHI
THWACK!

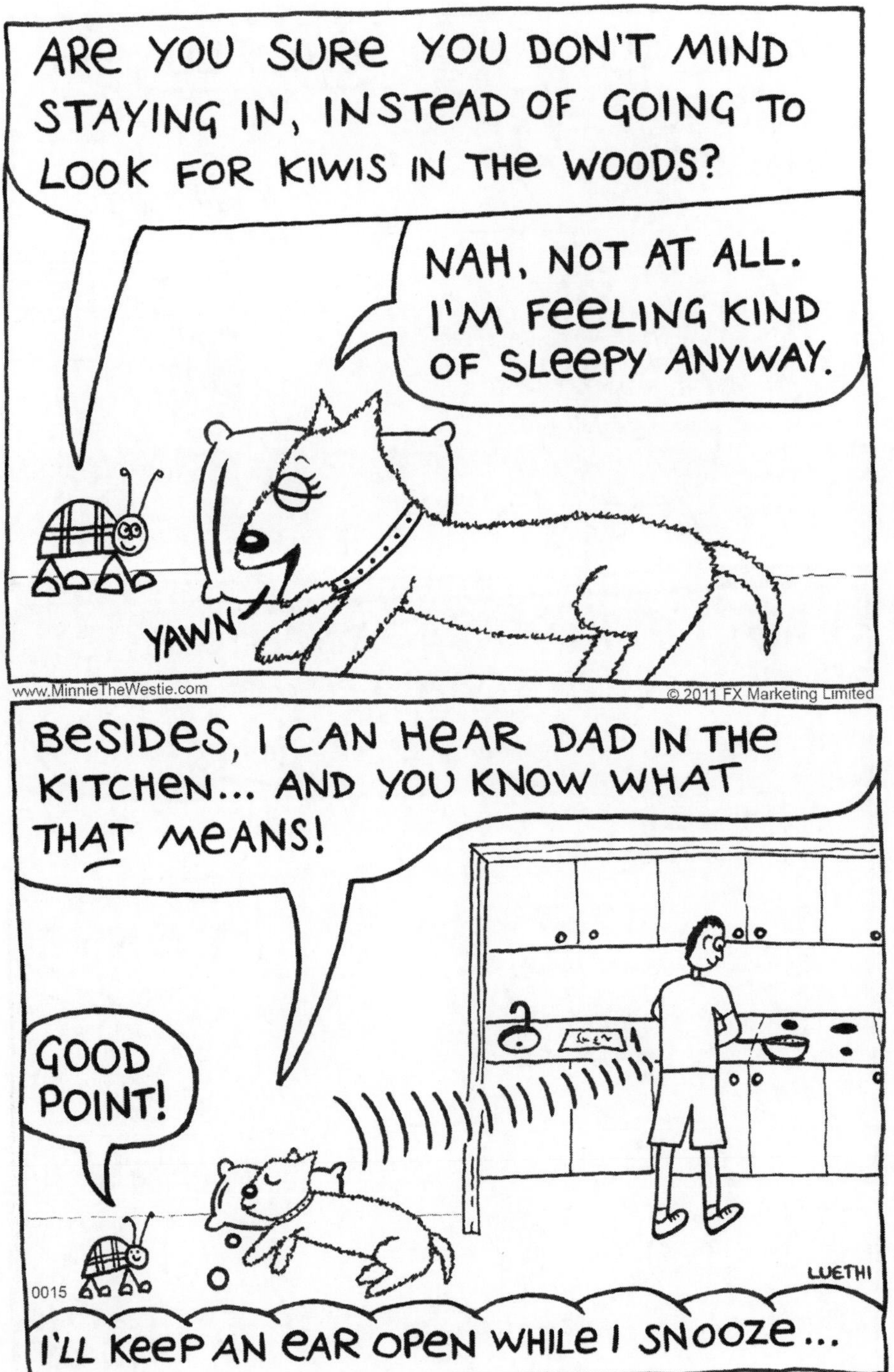
ARE YOU SURE YOU DON'T MIND STAYING IN, INSTEAD OF GOING TO LOOK FOR KIWIS IN THE WOODS?
NAH, NOT AT ALL. I'M FEELING KIND OF SLEEPY ANYWAY.
YAWN
www.MinnieTheWestie.com
© 2011 FX Marketing Limited
BESIDES, I CAN HEAR DAD IN THE KITCHEN... AND YOU KNOW WHAT THAT MEANS!
GOOD POINT!
LUETHI
0015
I'LL KEEP AN EAR OPEN WHILE I SNOOZE...

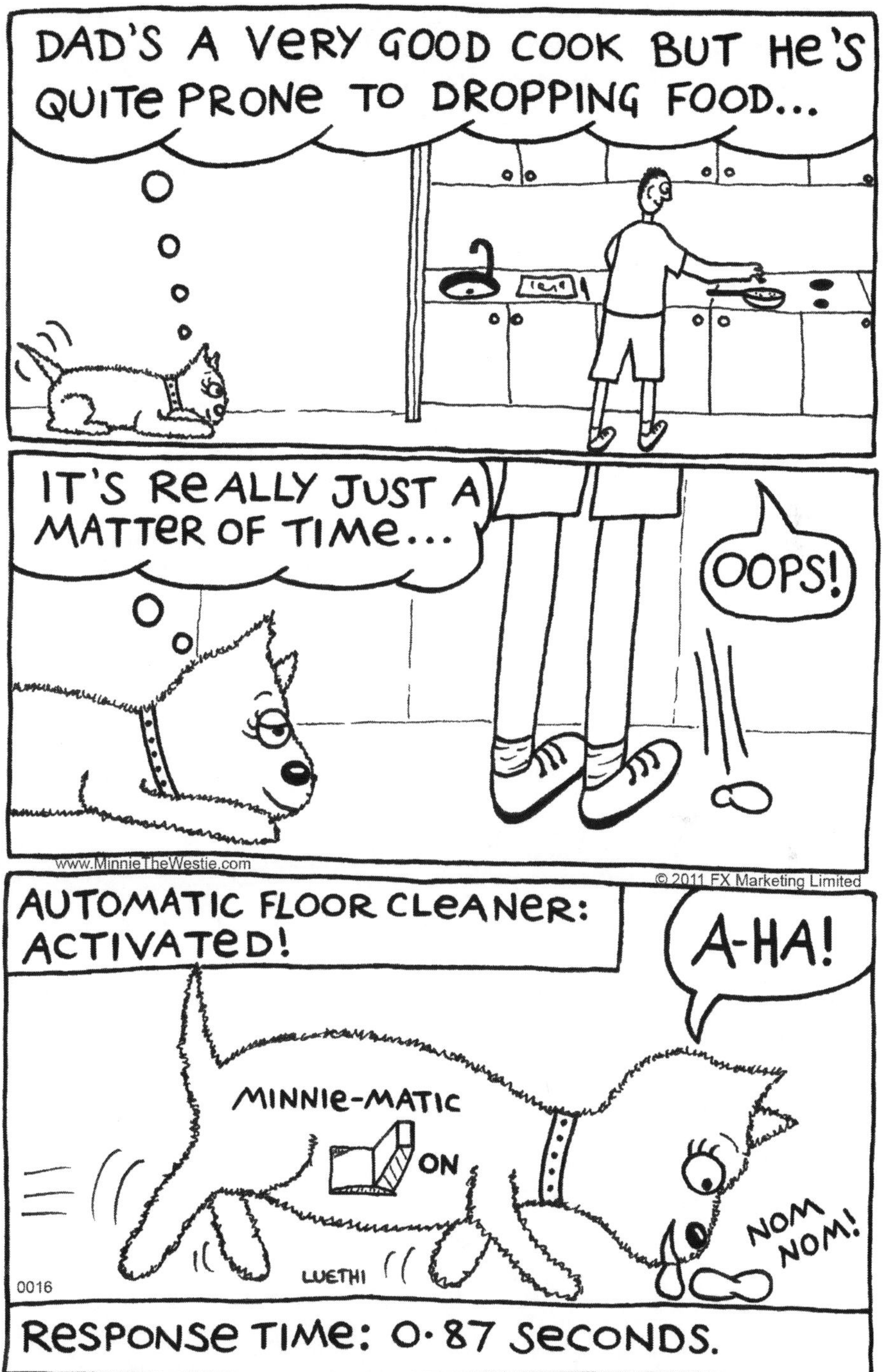
DAD'S A VERY GOOD COOK BUT HE'S QUITE PRONE TO DROPPING FOOD...
IT'S REALLY JUST A MATTER OF TIME...
OOPS!
www.MinnieTheWestie.com
© 2011 FX Marketing Limited
AUTOMATIC FLOOR CLEANER: ACTIVATED!
A-HA!
MINNIE-MATIC
ON
NOM NOM!
LUETHI
0016
RESPONSE TIME: 0·87 SECONDS.

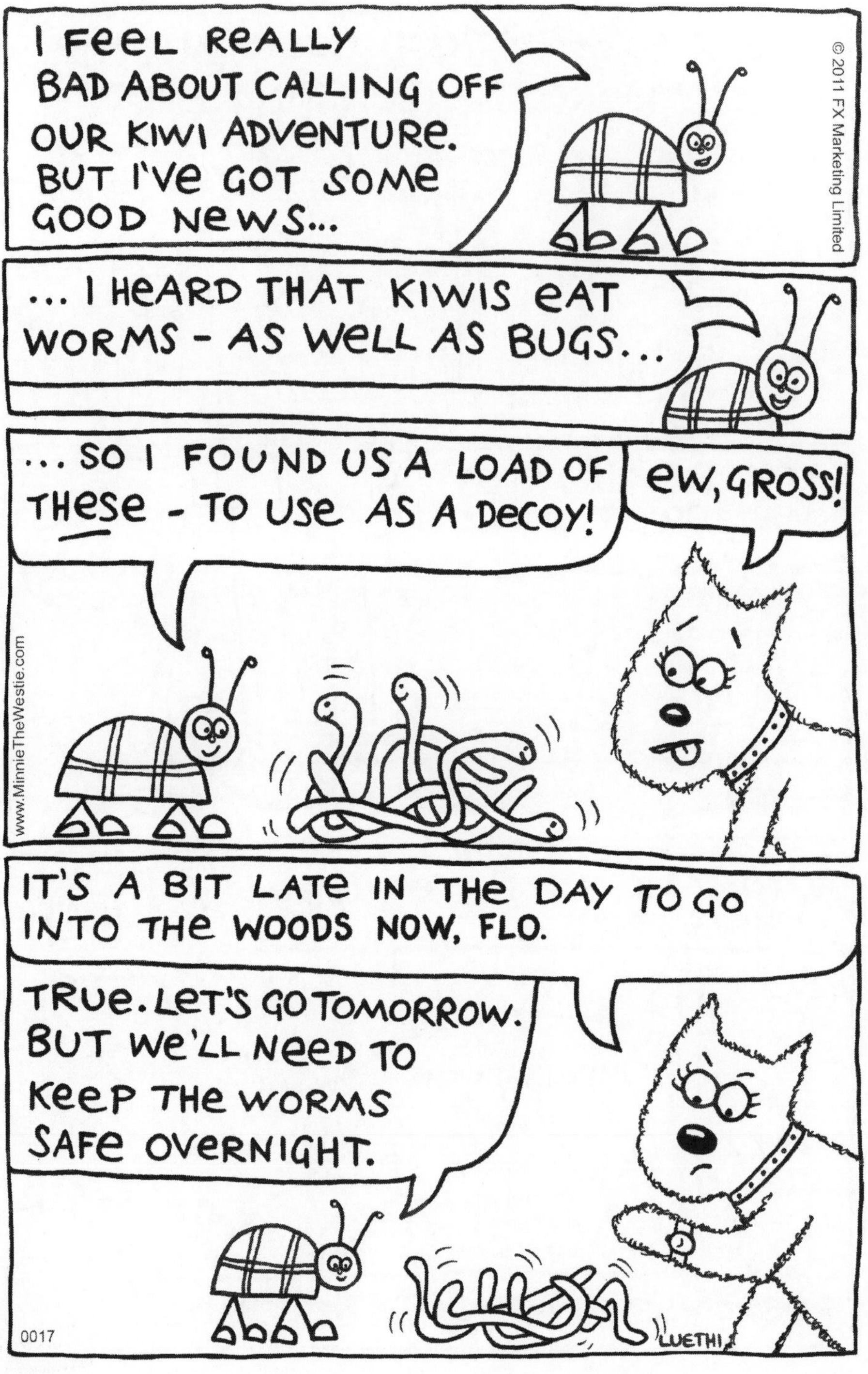
I FEEL REALLY BAD ABOUT CALLING OFF OUR KIWI ADVENTURE. BUT I'VE GOT SOME GOOD NEWS...
... I HEARD THAT KIWIS EAT WORMS - AS WELL AS BUGS...
... SO I FOUND US A LOAD OF THESE - TO USE AS A DECOY!
EW, GROSS!
IT'S A BIT LATE IN THE DAY TO GO INTO THE WOODS NOW, FLO.
TRUE. LET'S GO TOMORROW. BUT WE'LL NEED TO KEEP THE WORMS SAFE OVERNIGHT.
© 2011 FX Marketing Limited
www.MinnieTheWestie.com
0017
LUETHI

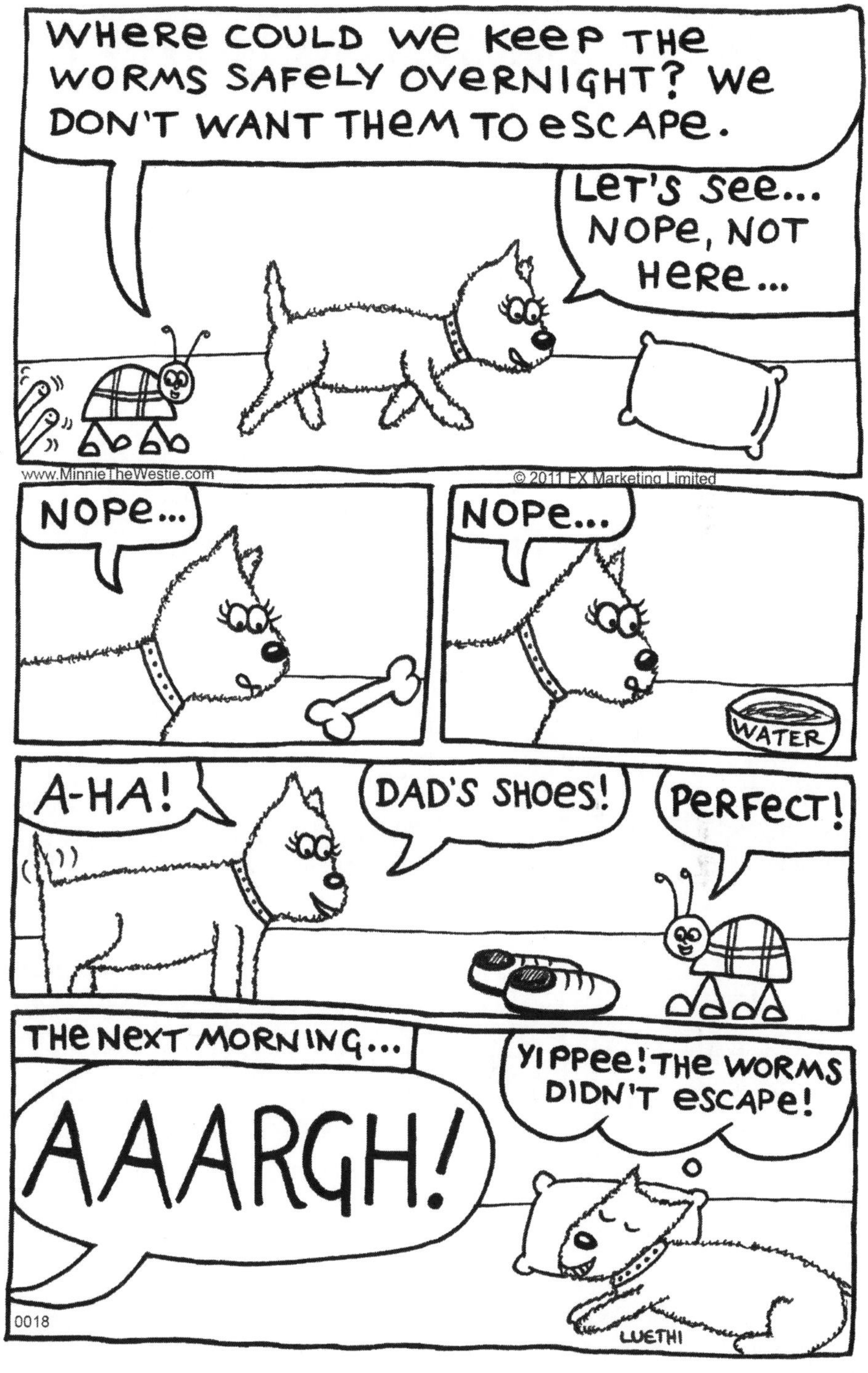

WHERE COULD WE KEEP THE WORMS SAFELY OVERNIGHT? WE DON'T WANT THEM TO ESCAPE.
LET'S SEE... NOPE, NOT HERE...
www.MinnieTheWestie.com
© 2011 FX Marketing Limited
NOPE...
NOPE...
WATER
A-HA!
DAD'S SHOES!
PERFECT!
THE NEXT MORNING...
AAARGH!
YIPPEE! THE WORMS DIDN'T ESCAPE!
0018
LUETHI

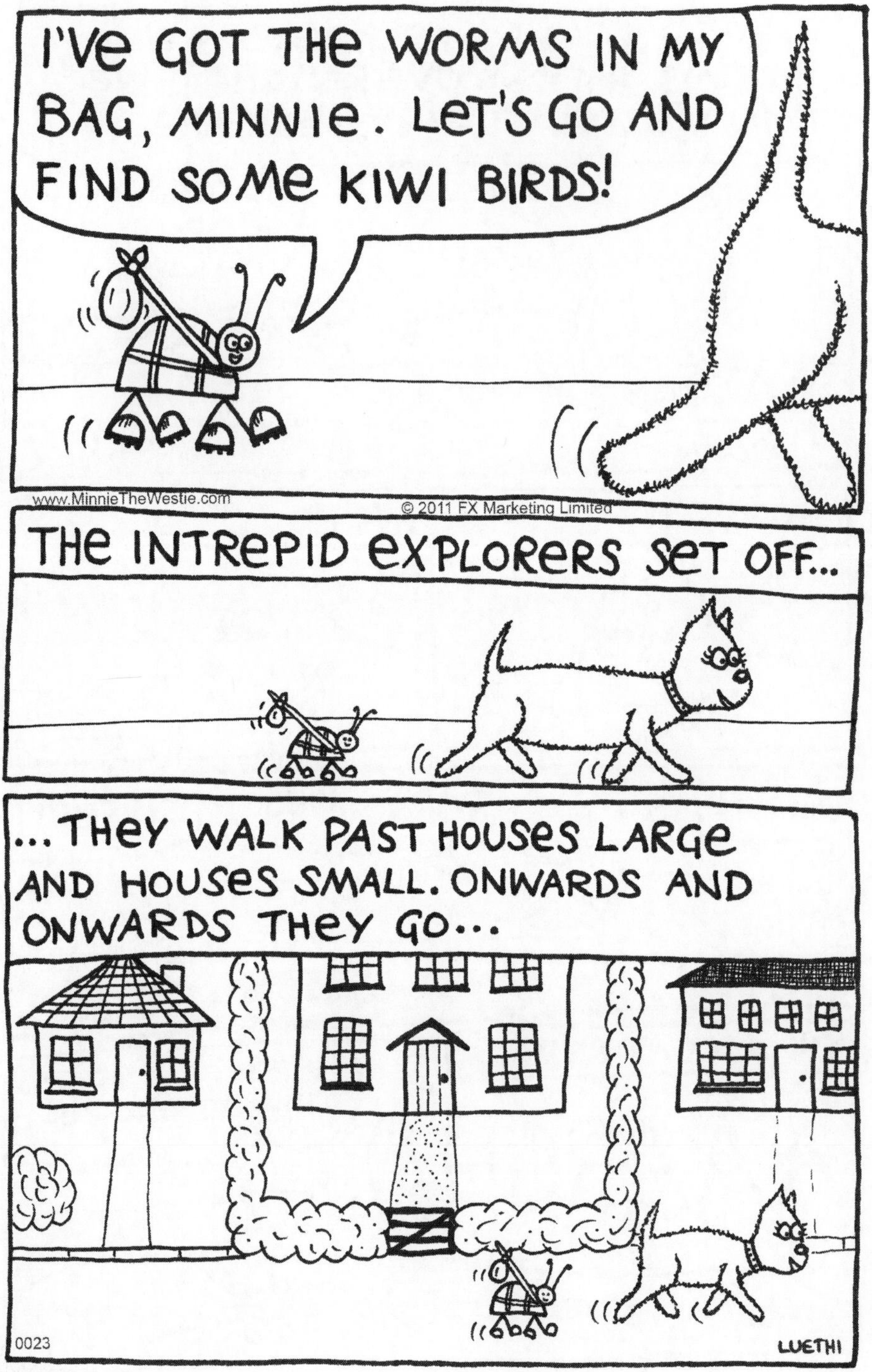
I'VE GOT THE WORMS IN MY BAG, MINNIE. LET'S GO AND FIND SOME KIWI BIRDS!
www.MinnieTheWestie.com
© 2011 FX Marketing Limited
THE INTREPID EXPLORERS SET OFF...
...THEY WALK PAST HOUSES LARGE AND HOUSES SMALL. ONWARDS AND ONWARDS THEY GO...
0023
LUETHI

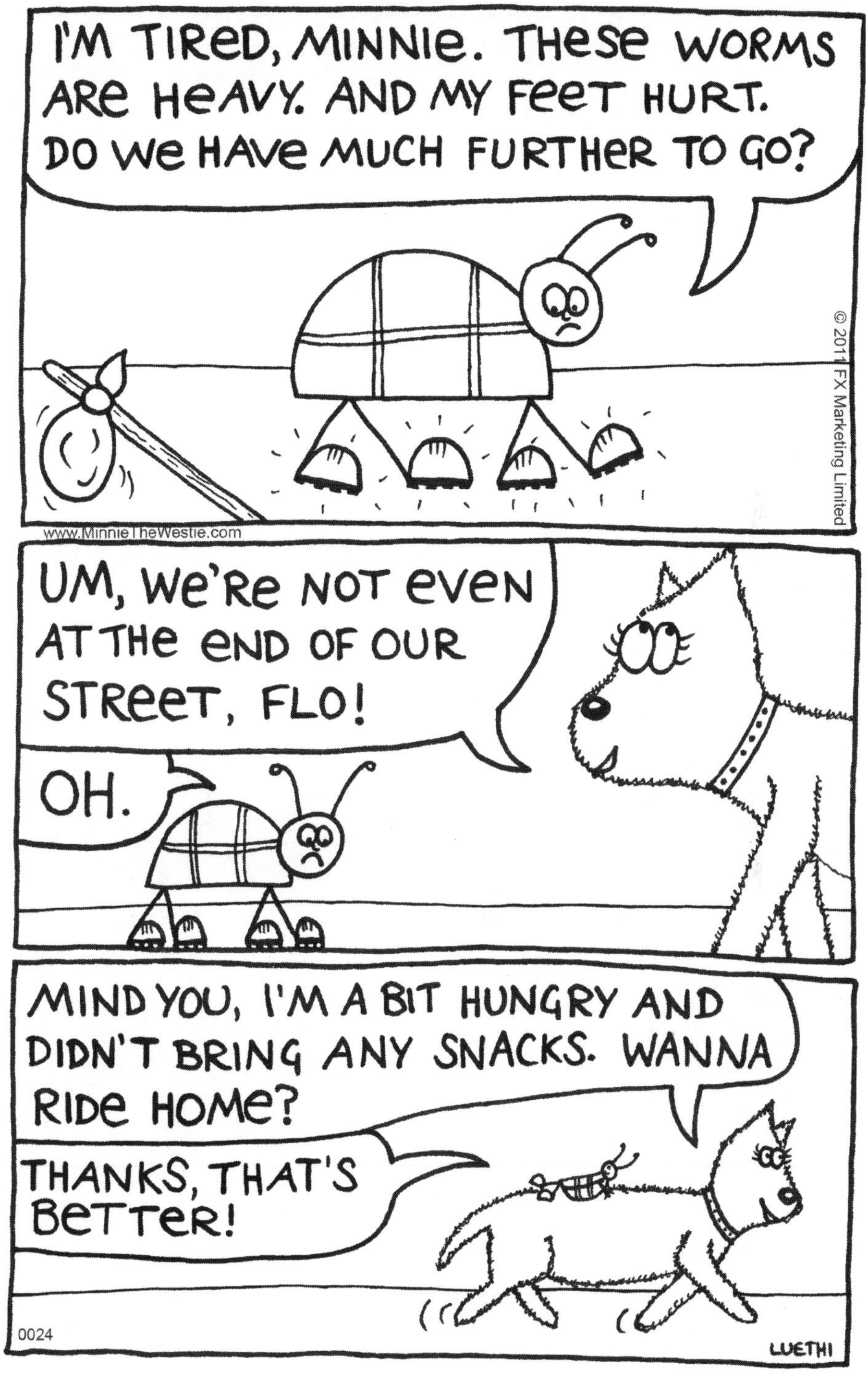
I'M TIRED, MINNIE. THESE WORMS ARE HEAVY. AND MY FEET HURT. DO WE HAVE MUCH FURTHER TO GO?
© 2011 FX Marketing Limited
www.MinnieTheWestie.com
UM, WE'RE NOT EVEN AT THE END OF OUR STREET, FLO!
OH.
MIND YOU, I'M A BIT HUNGRY AND DIDN'T BRING ANY SNACKS. WANNA RIDE HOME?
THANKS, THAT'S BETTER!
0024
LUETHI

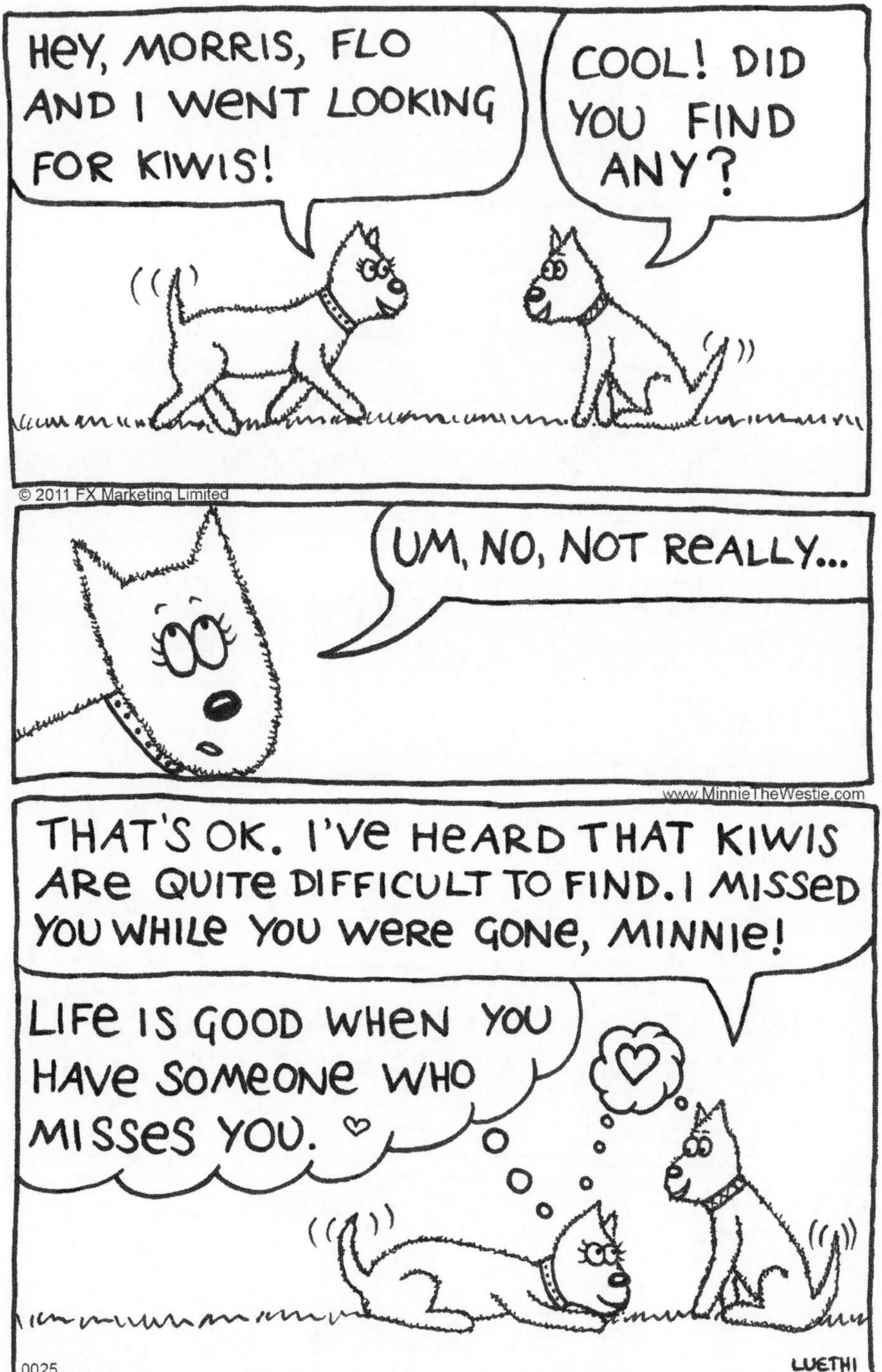
HEY, MORRIS, FLO AND I WENT LOOKING FOR KIWIS!
COOL! DID YOU FIND ANY?
© 2011 FX Marketing Limited
UM, NO, NOT REALLY...
www.MinnieTheWestie.com
THAT'S OK. I'VE HEARD THAT KIWIS ARE QUITE DIFFICULT TO FIND. I MISSED YOU WHILE YOU WERE GONE, MINNIE!
LIFE IS GOOD WHEN YOU HAVE SOMEONE WHO MISSES YOU.
0025
LUETHI

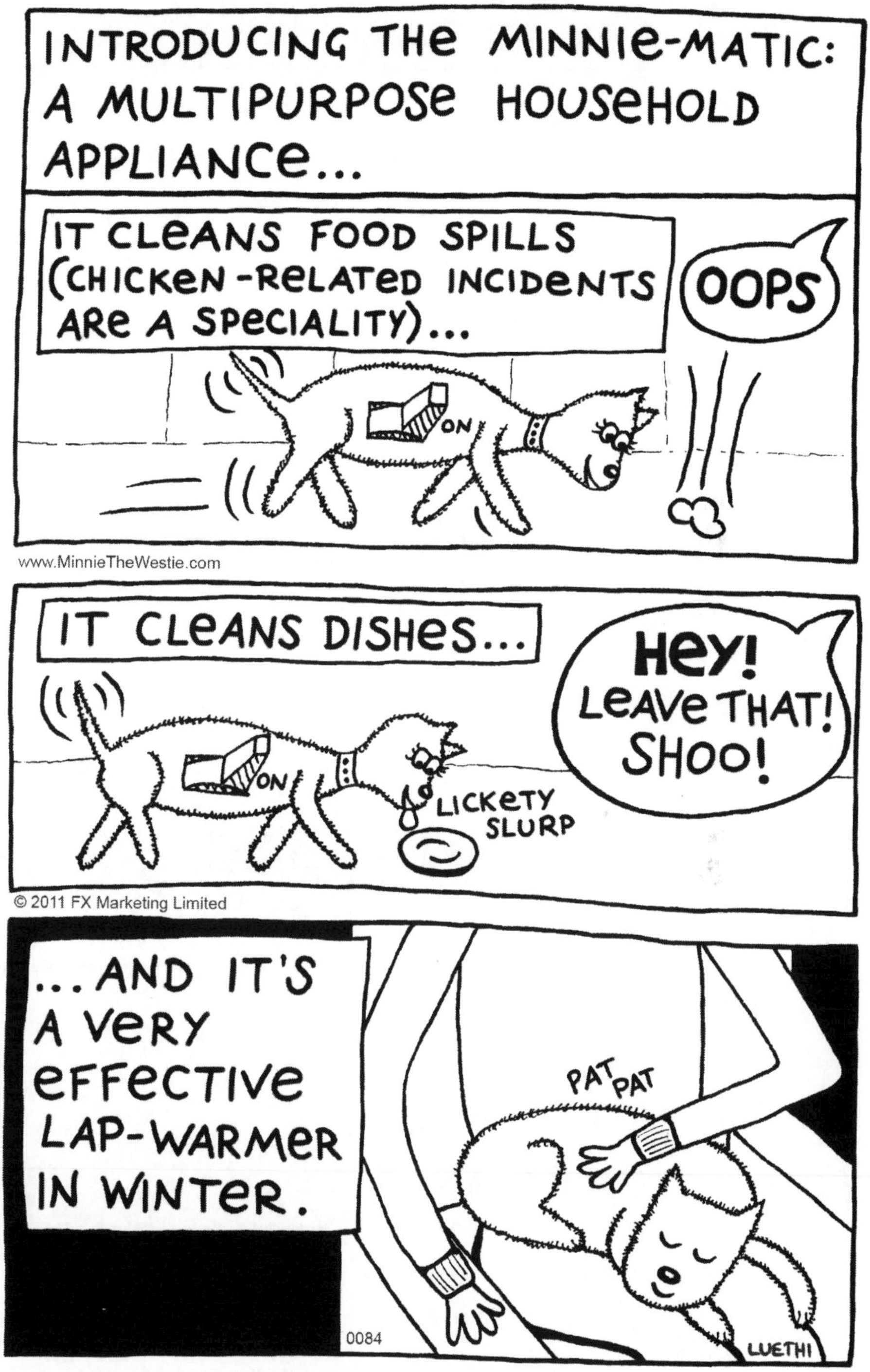
INTRODUCING THE MINNIE-MATIC: A MULTIPURPOSE HOUSEHOLD APPLIANCE...
IT CLEANS FOOD SPILLS (CHICKEN-RELATED INCIDENTS ARE A SPECIALITY)...
OOPS
ON
www.MinnieTheWestie.com
IT CLEANS DISHES...
HEY! LEAVE THAT! SHOO!
ON
LICKETY SLURP
© 2011 FX Marketing Limited
...AND IT'S A VERY EFFECTIVE LAP-WARMER IN WINTER.
PAT PAT
0084
LUETHI

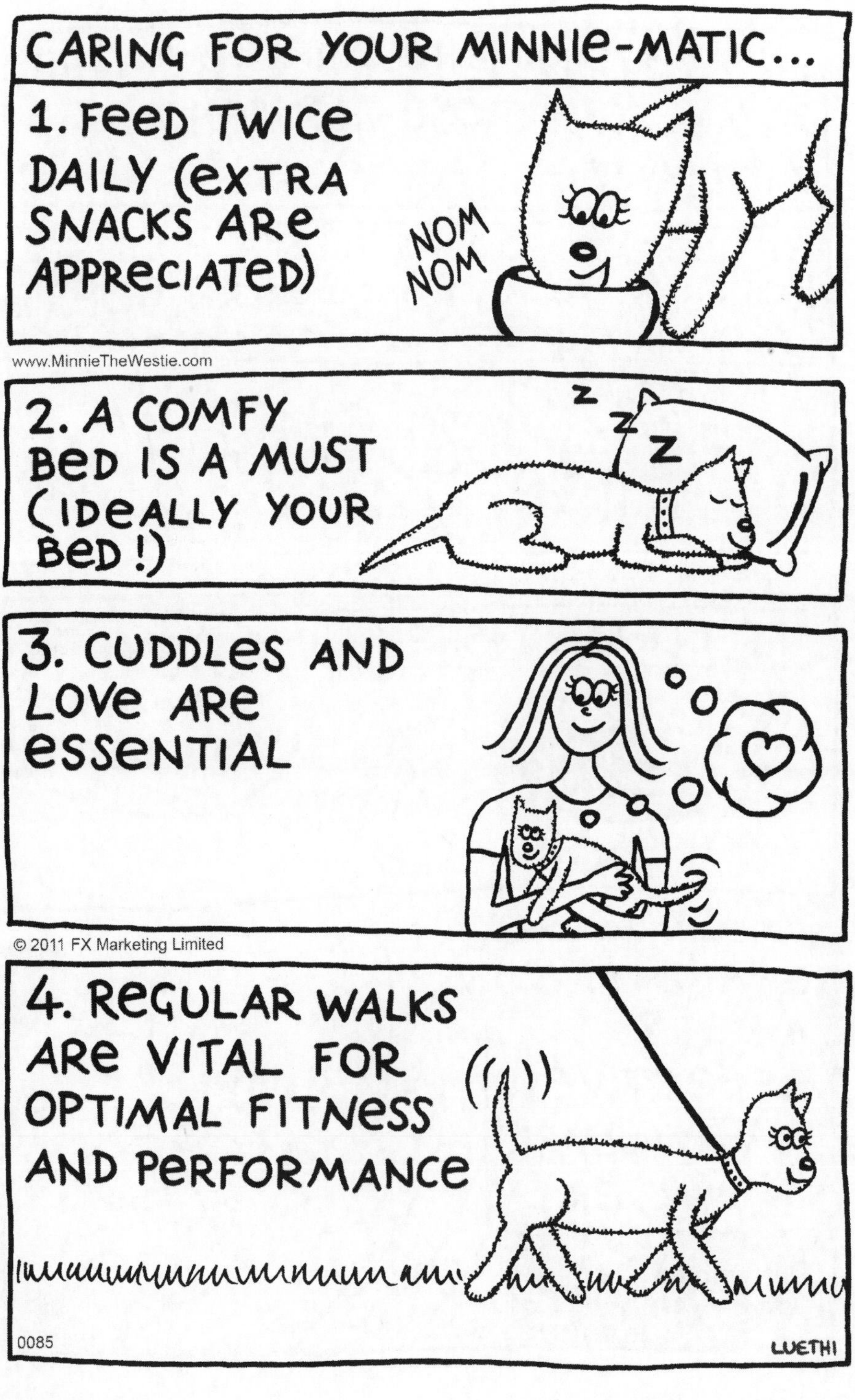
CARING FOR YOUR MINNIE-MATIC...
1. FEED TWICE DAILY (EXTRA SNACKS ARE APPRECIATED)
NOM NOM
2. A COMFY BED IS A MUST (IDEALLY YOUR BED!)
Z Z Z
3. CUDDLES AND LOVE ARE ESSENTIAL
4. REGULAR WALKS ARE VITAL FOR OPTIMAL FITNESS AND PERFORMANCE
0085
LUETHI

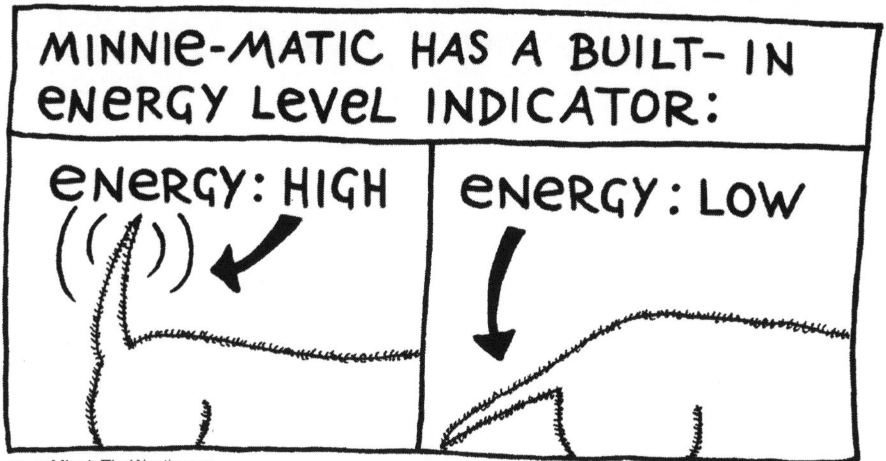
MINNIE-MATIC HAS A BUILT-IN ENERGY LEVEL INDICATOR:
ENERGY: HIGH
ENERGY: LOW

www.MinnieTheWestie.com

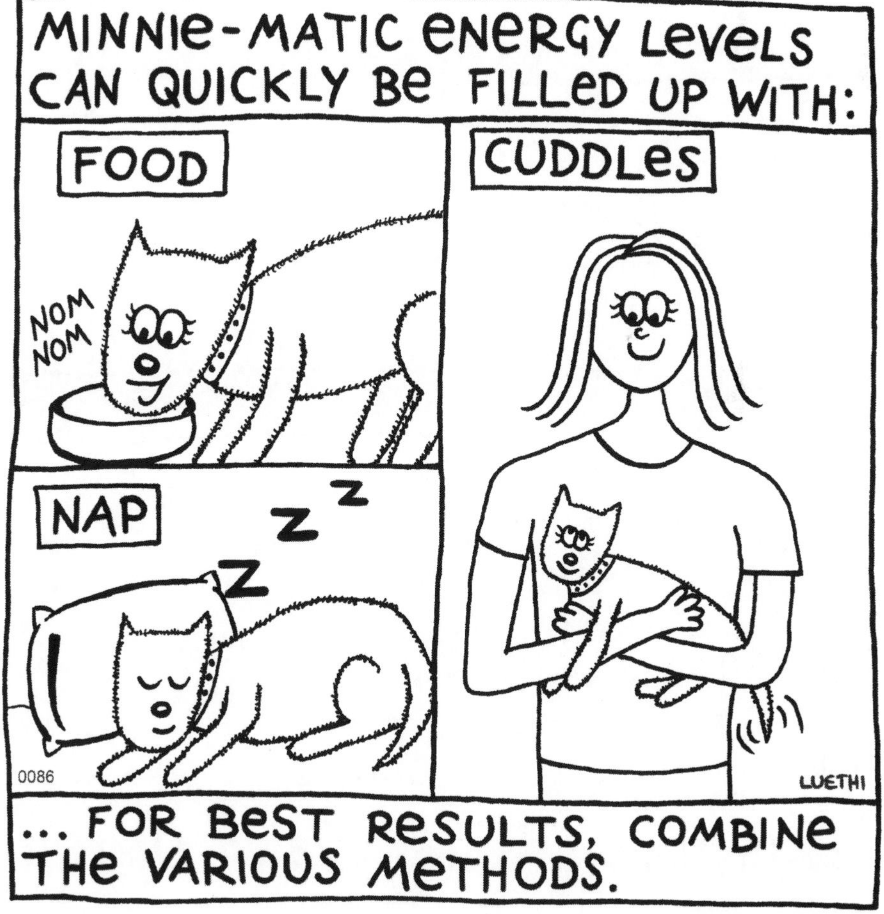
MINNIE-MATIC ENERGY LEVELS CAN QUICKLY BE FILLED UP WITH:
FOOD
NOM NOM
CUDDLES
NAP
Z Z Z
0086
LUETHI
... FOR BEST RESULTS, COMBINE THE VARIOUS METHODS.

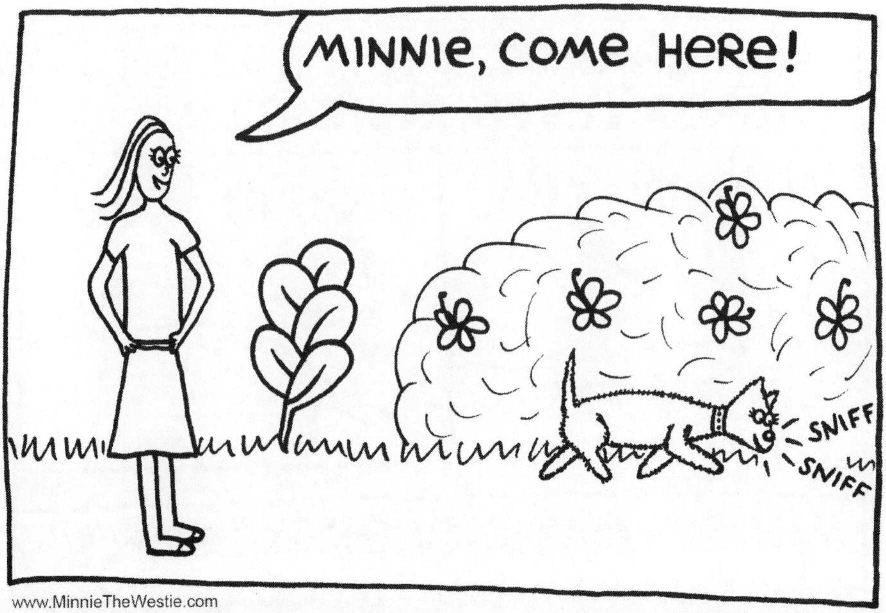
MINNIE, COME HERE!
SNIFF
SNIFF

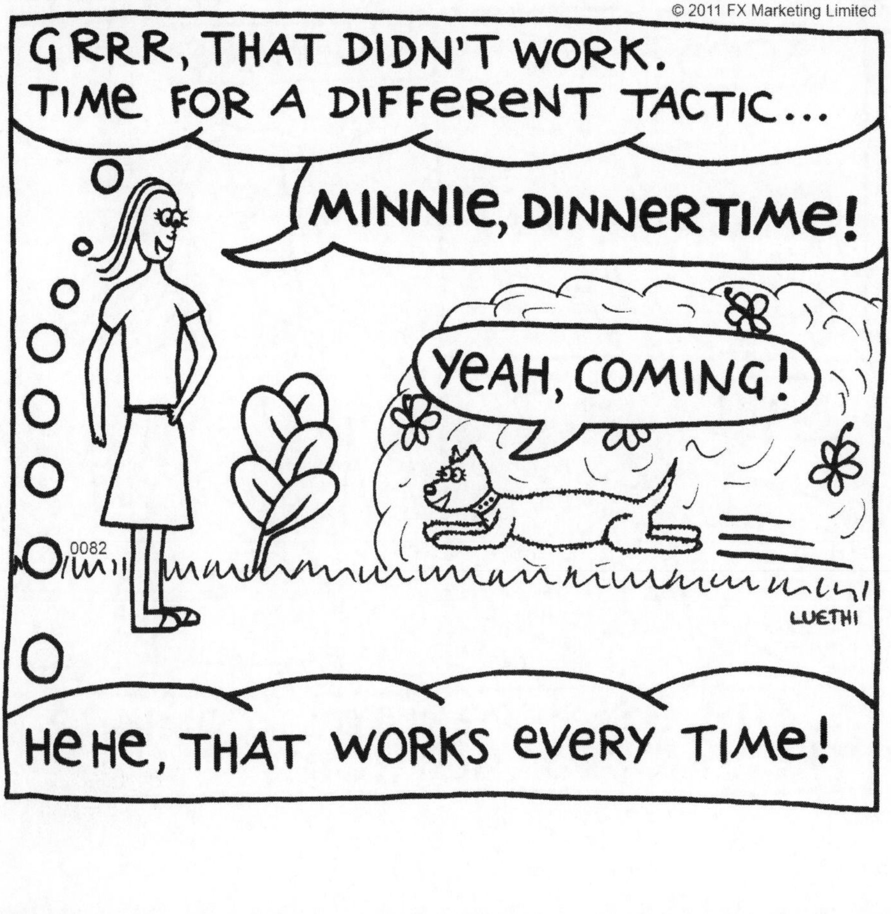
GRRR, THAT DIDN'T WORK.
TIME FOR A DIFFERENT TACTIC...
MINNIE, DINNERTIME!
YEAH, COMING!
0082
LUETHI
HEHE, THAT WORKS EVERY TIME!

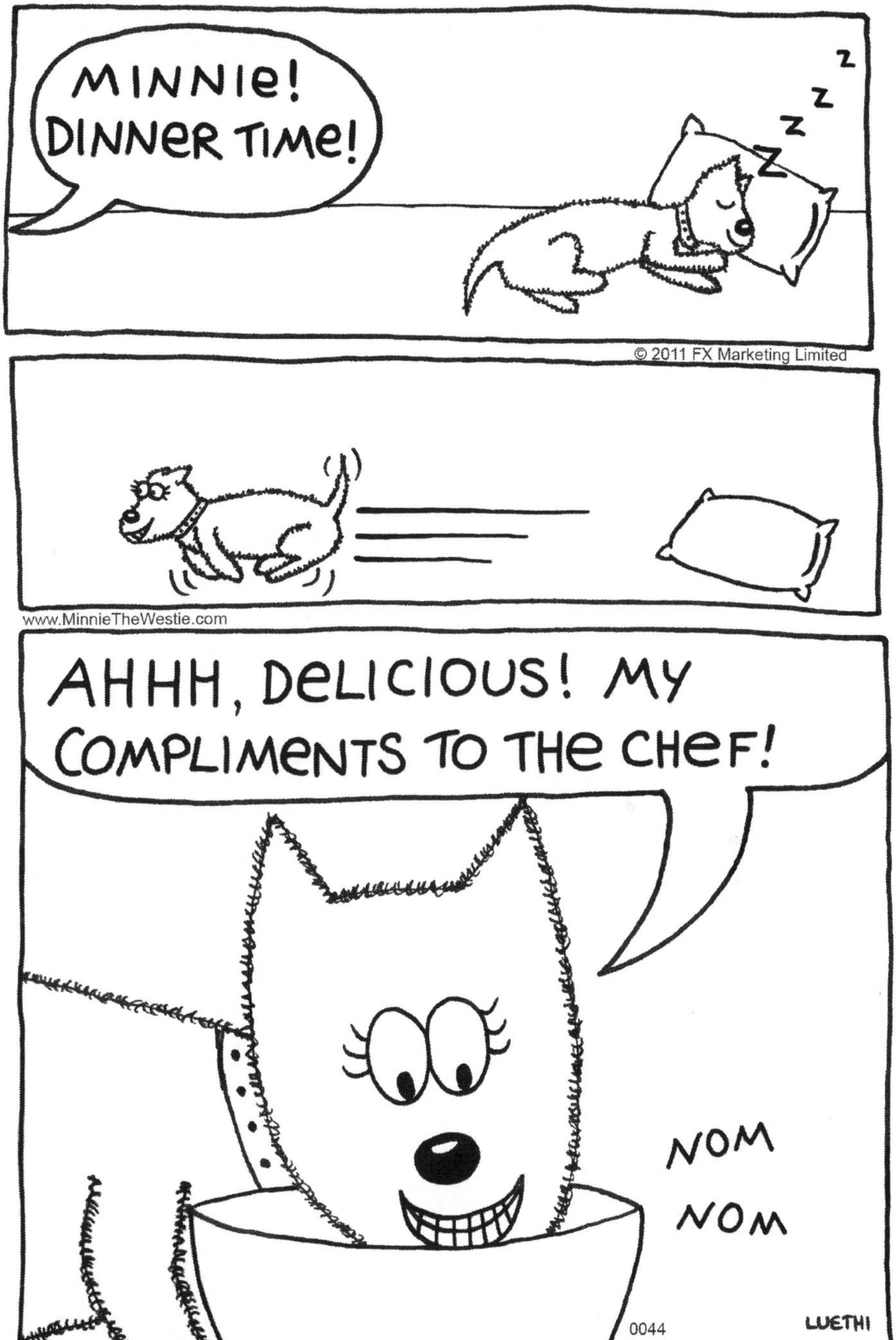
MINNIE! DINNER TIME!
Z Z Z Z
© 2011 FX Marketing Limited
www.MinnieTheWestie.com
AHHH, DELICIOUS! MY COMPLIMENTS TO THE CHEF!
NOM NOM
0044
LUETHI

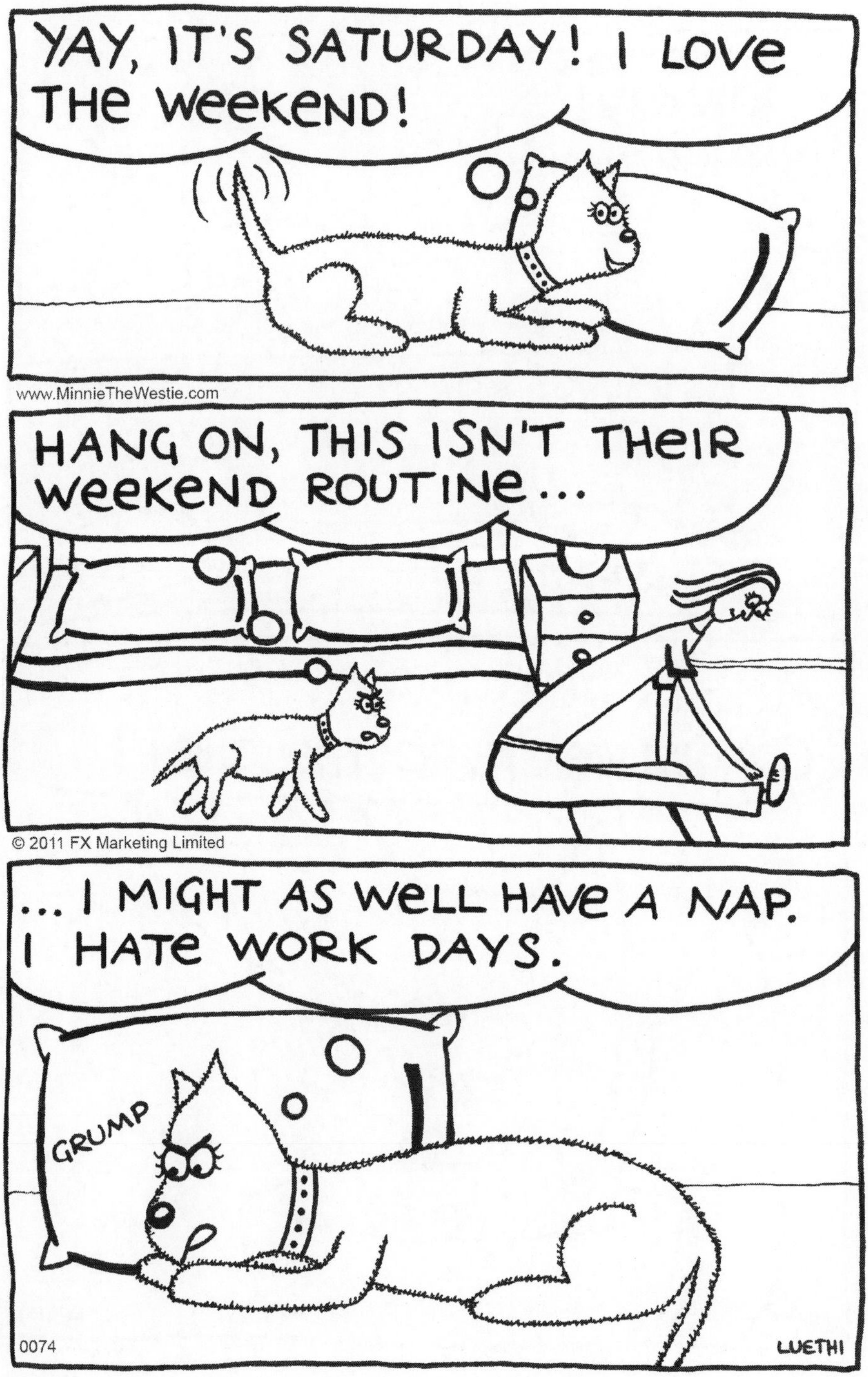
YAY, IT'S SATURDAY! I LOVE THE WEEKEND!
HANG ON, THIS ISN'T THEIR WEEKEND ROUTINE...
... I MIGHT AS WELL HAVE A NAP. I HATE WORK DAYS.
GRUMP
0074
LUETHI

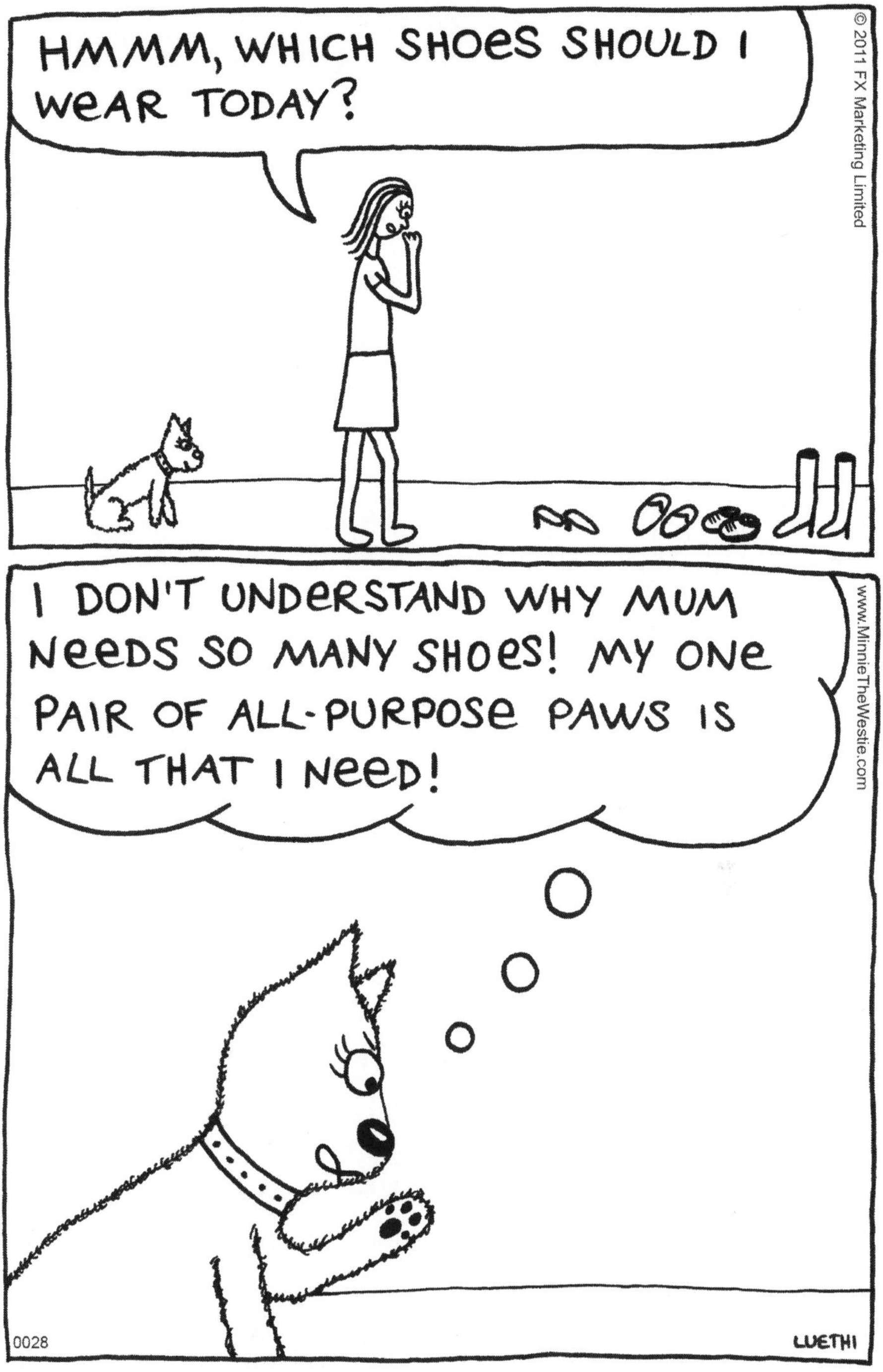
HMMM, WHICH SHOES SHOULD I WEAR TODAY?
I DON'T UNDERSTAND WHY MUM NEEDS SO MANY SHOES! MY ONE PAIR OF ALL-PURPOSE PAWS IS ALL THAT I NEED!
© 2011 FX Marketing Limited
www.MinnieTheWestie.com
0028
LUETHI

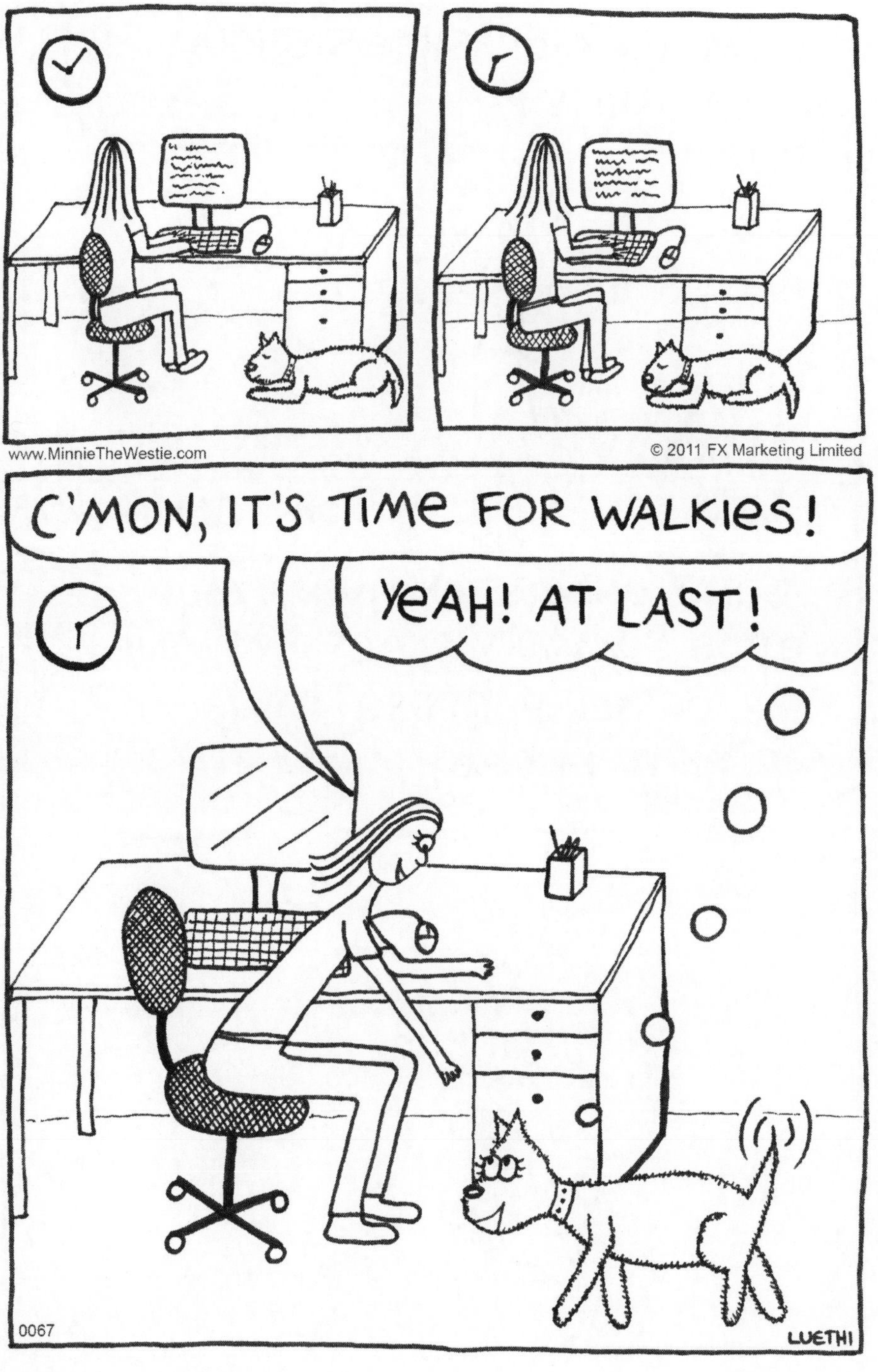
www.MinnieTheWestie.com
© 2011 FX Marketing Limited
C'MON, IT'S TIME FOR WALKIES!
YEAH! AT LAST!
0067
LUETHI

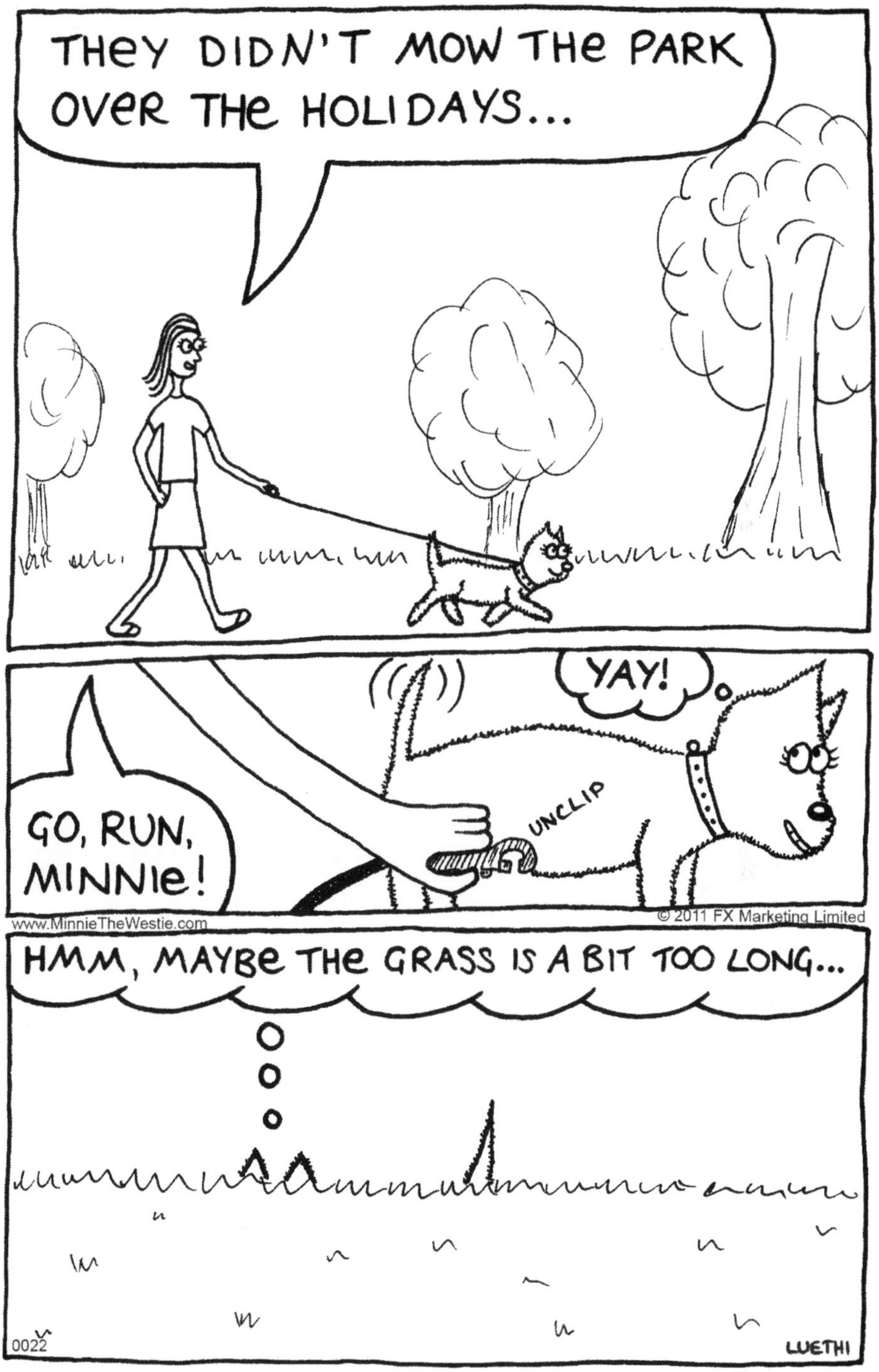
THEY DIDN'T MOW THE PARK OVER THE HOLIDAYS...
YAY!
GO, RUN, MINNIE!
UNCLIP
www.MinnieTheWestie.com
© 2011 FX Marketing Limited
HMM, MAYBE THE GRASS IS A BIT TOO LONG...
0022
LUETHI

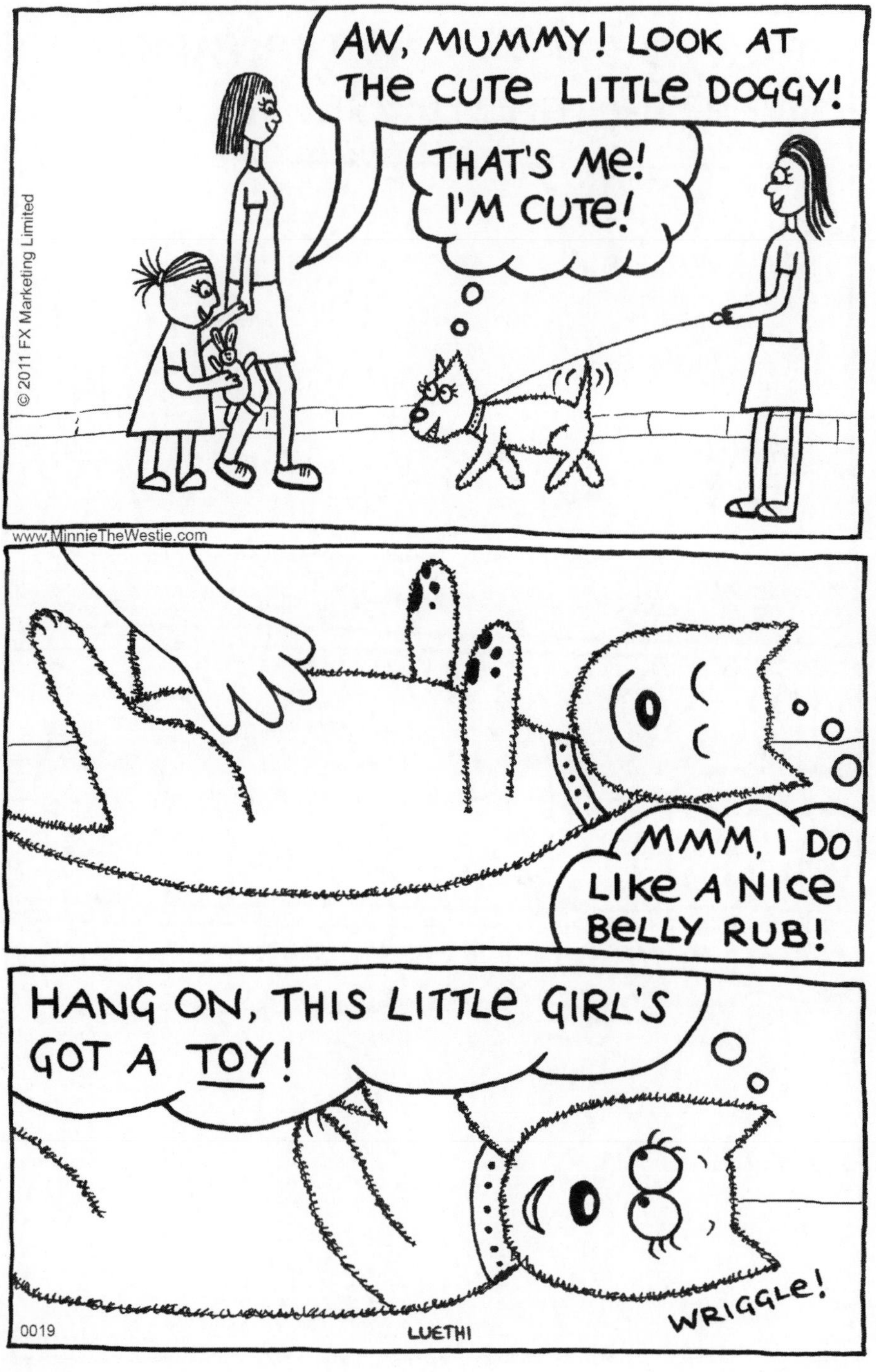
AW, MUMMY! LOOK AT THE CUTE LITTLE DOGGY!
THAT'S ME! I'M CUTE!
© 2011 FX Marketing Limited
www.MinnieTheWestie.com
MMM, I DO LIKE A NICE BELLY RUB!
HANG ON, THIS LITTLE GIRL'S GOT A TOY!
WRIGGLE!
0019
LUETHI

THANKS FOR THE TOY BUNNY, LITTLE GIRL. I LIKE!
WAAAAH!
SORRY, LITTLE GIRL. IT WAS A MISUNDERSTANDING. MY MISTAKE. HERE'S YOUR TOY BUNNY.
YAY, BUNNY! NICE DOGGY!
PTOO!
0020
LUETHI

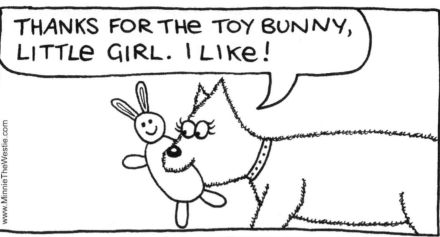

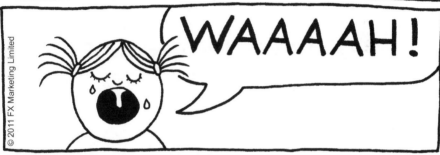

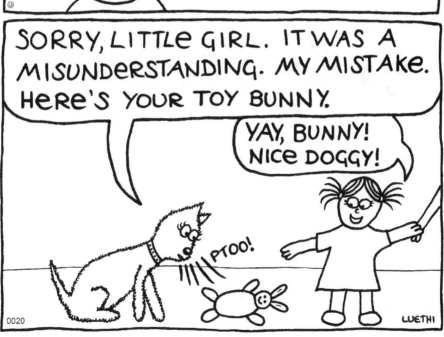

SNAP
SNAP
www.MinnieTheWestie.com
I HATE ALL THE FLIES AT THIS TIME OF YEAR. THEY'RE BUGGING ME!
SNAP
SNAP
© 2011 FX Marketing Limited
EW, GROSS! I ACTUALLY CAUGHT ONE!
PTOO
0064
LUETHI

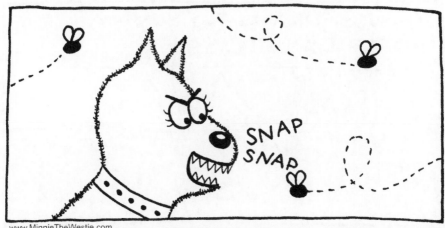

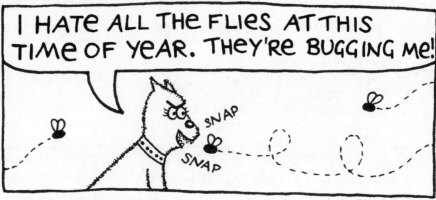

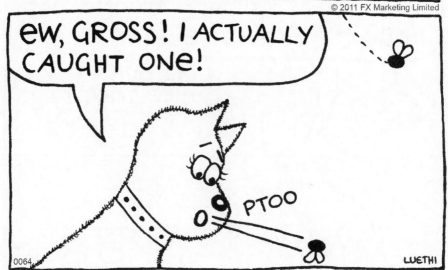

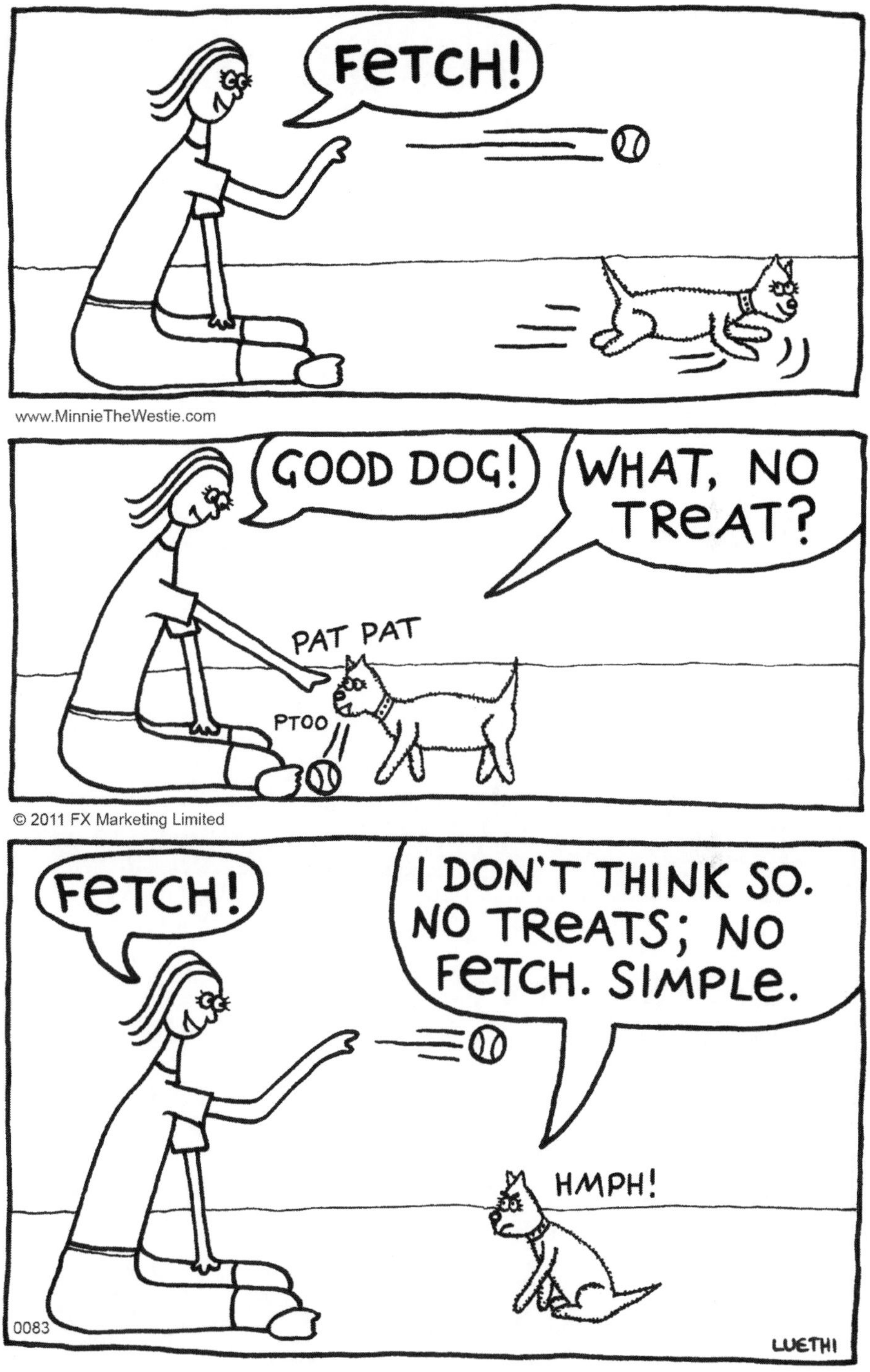
FETCH!
GOOD DOG!
WHAT, NO TREAT?
PAT PAT
PTOO
FETCH!
I DON'T THINK SO. NO TREATS; NO FETCH. SIMPLE.
HMPH!
0083
LUETHI

www.MinnieTheWestie.com

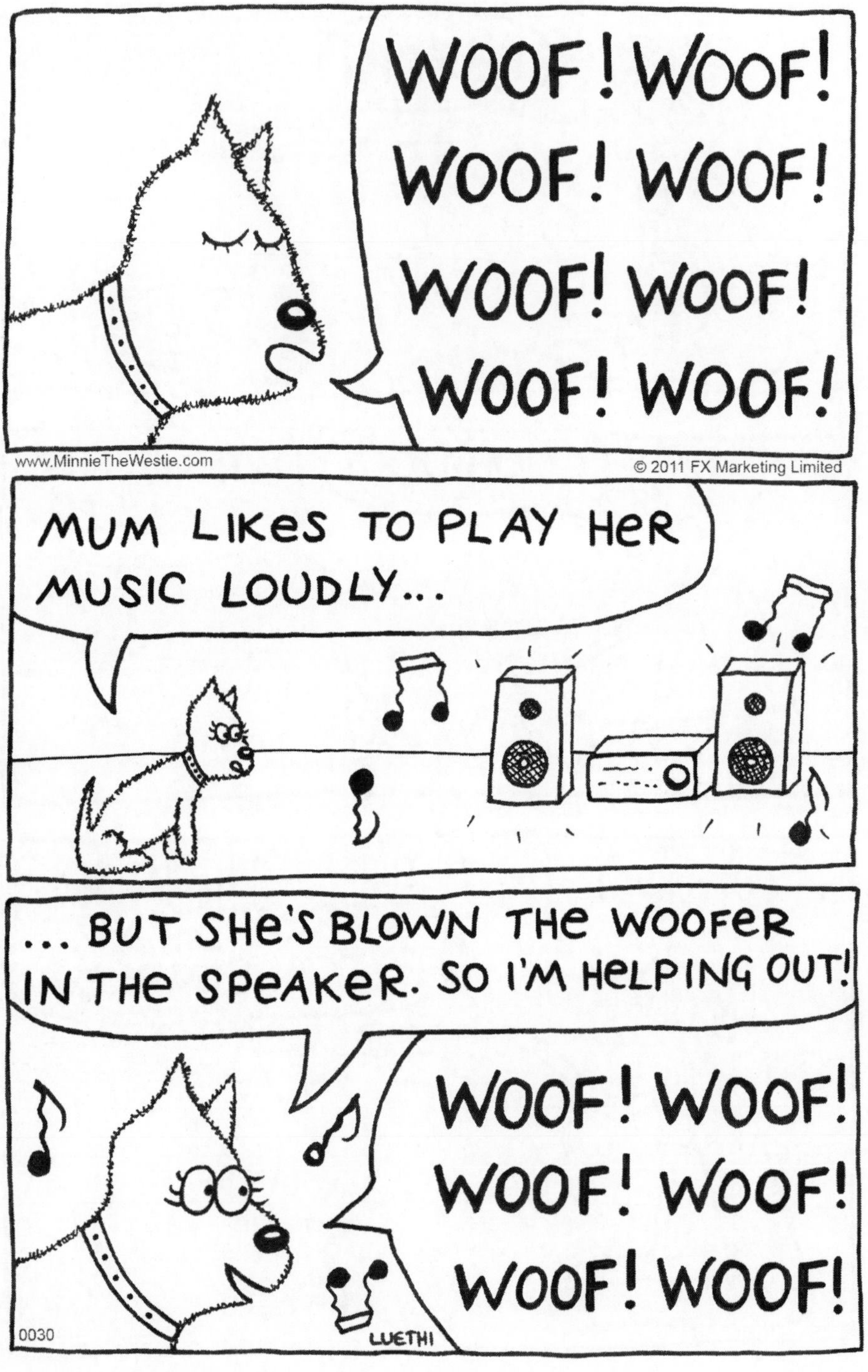
WOOF! WOOF! WOOF! WOOF! WOOF! WOOF! WOOF! WOOF!
MUM LIKES TO PLAY HER MUSIC LOUDLY...
... BUT SHE'S BLOWN THE WOOFER IN THE SPEAKER. SO I'M HELPING OUT!
WOOF! WOOF! WOOF! WOOF! WOOF! WOOF!
LUETHI
0030

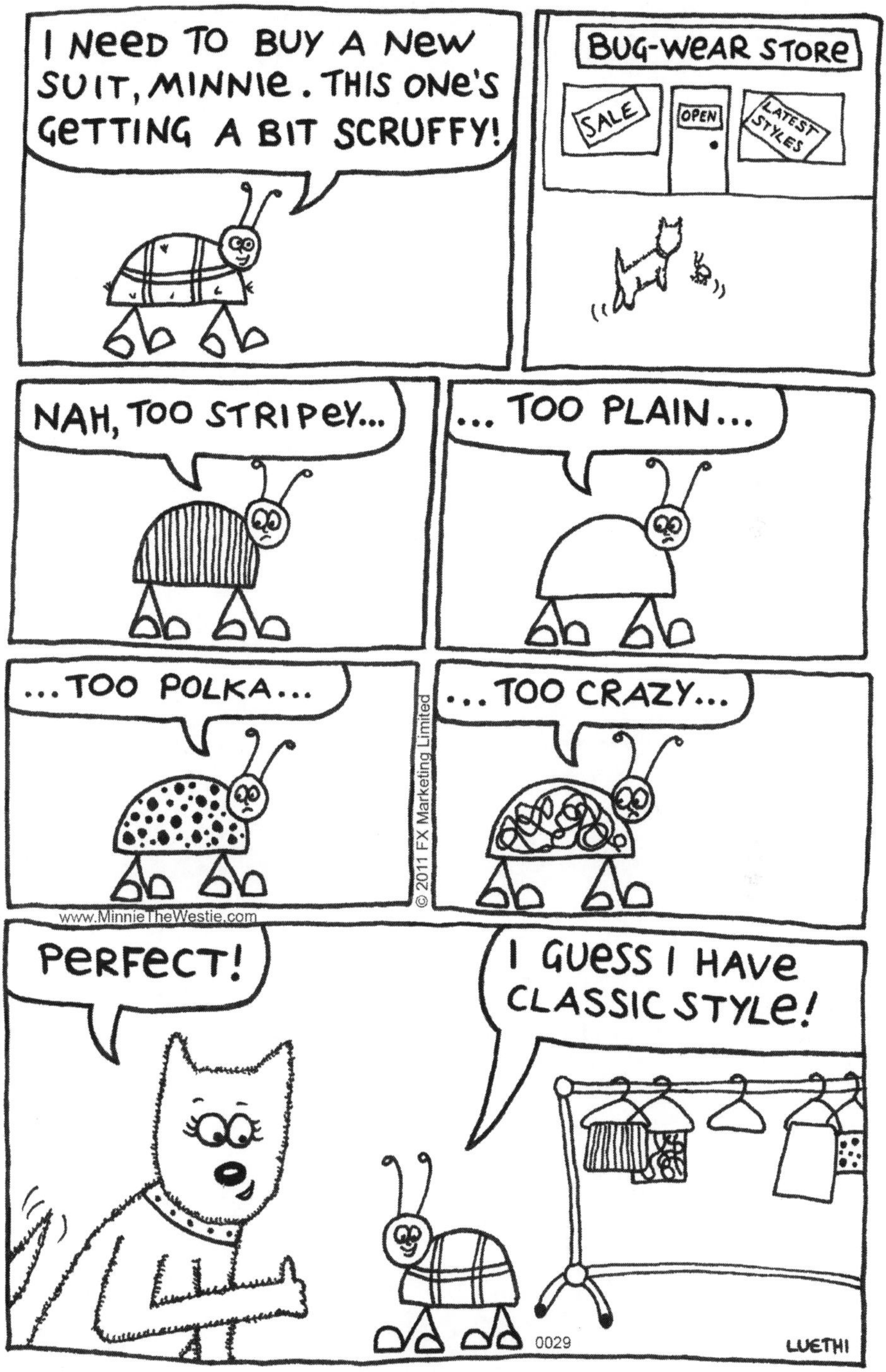
I NEED TO BUY A NEW SUIT, MINNIE. THIS ONE'S GETTING A BIT SCRUFFY!
BUG-WEAR STORE
SALE
OPEN
LATEST STYLES
NAH, TOO STRIPEY...
... TOO PLAIN...
...TOO POLKA...
...TOO CRAZY...
© 2011 FX Marketing Limited
www.MinnieTheWestie.com
PERFECT!
I GUESS I HAVE CLASSIC STYLE!
0029
LUETHI

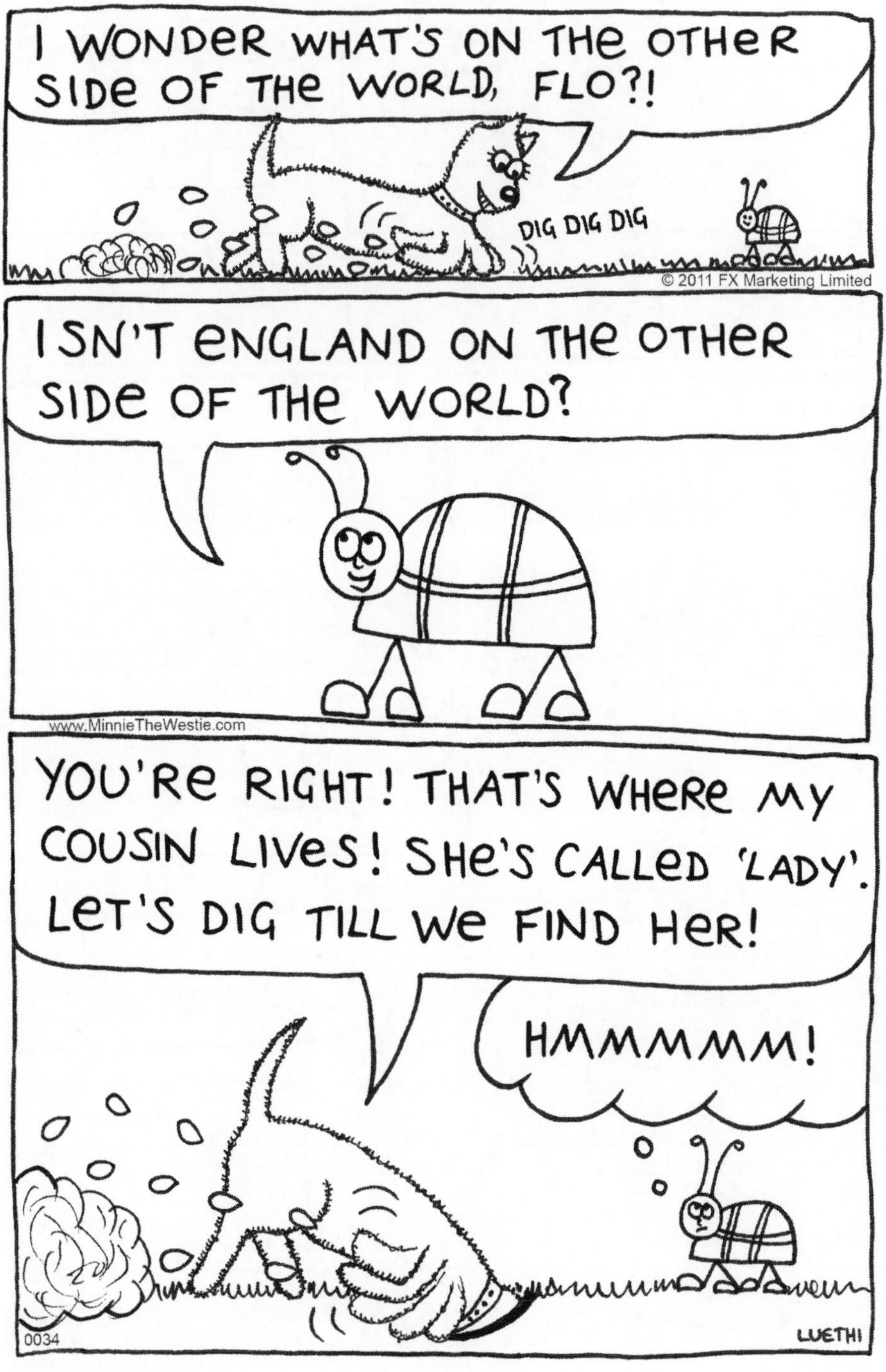
I WONDER WHAT'S ON THE OTHER SIDE OF THE WORLD, FLO?!
DIG DIG DIG
© 2011 FX Marketing Limited
ISN'T ENGLAND ON THE OTHER SIDE OF THE WORLD?
www.MinnieTheWestie.com
YOU'RE RIGHT! THAT'S WHERE MY COUSIN LIVES! SHE'S CALLED 'LADY'. LET'S DIG TILL WE FIND HER!
HMMMMM!
0034
LUETHI

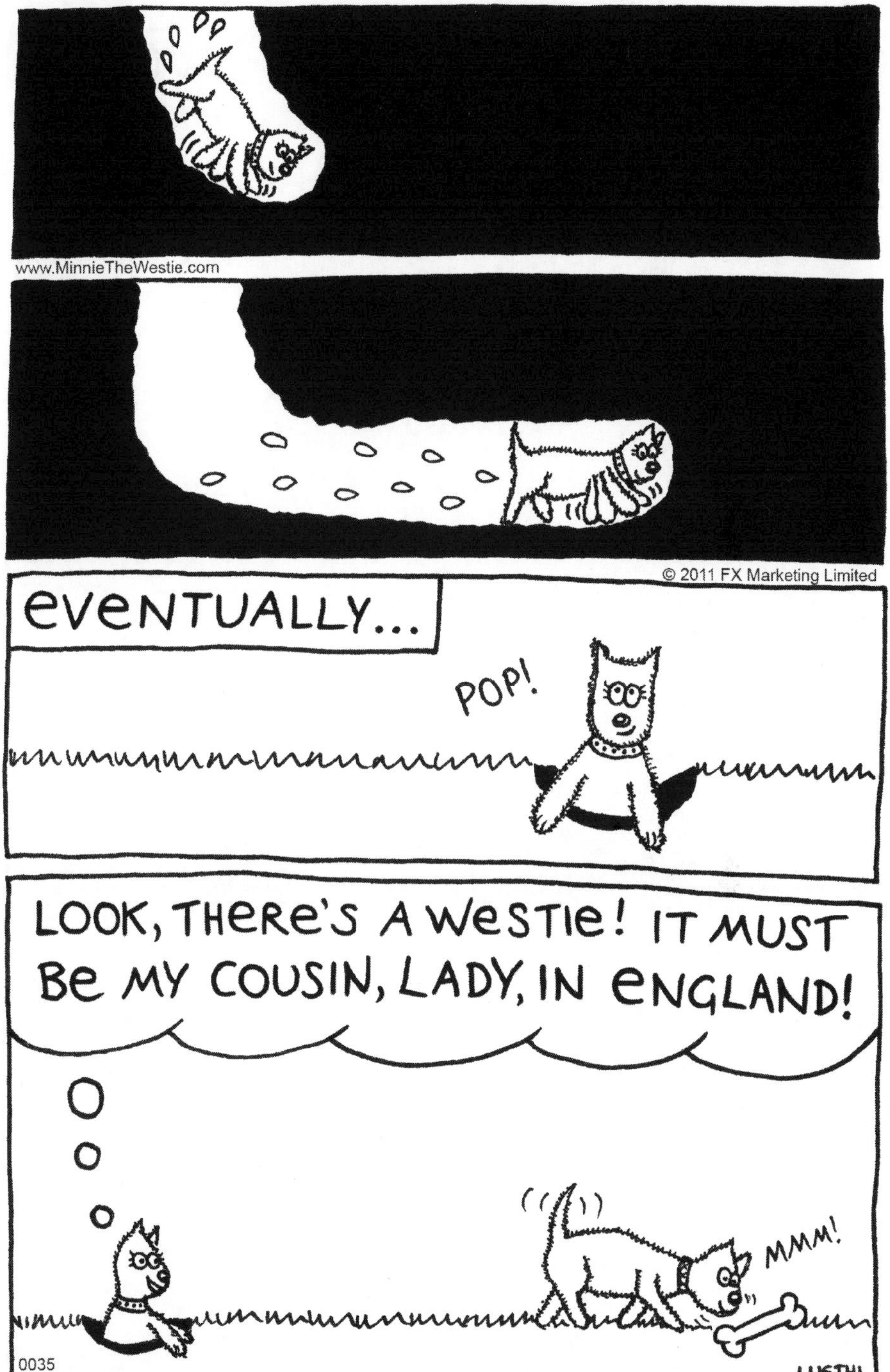
www.MinnieTheWestie.com
© 2011 FX Marketing Limited
EVENTUALLY...
POP!
LOOK, THERE'S A WESTIE! IT MUST BE MY COUSIN, LADY, IN ENGLAND!
MMM!
0035
LUETHI

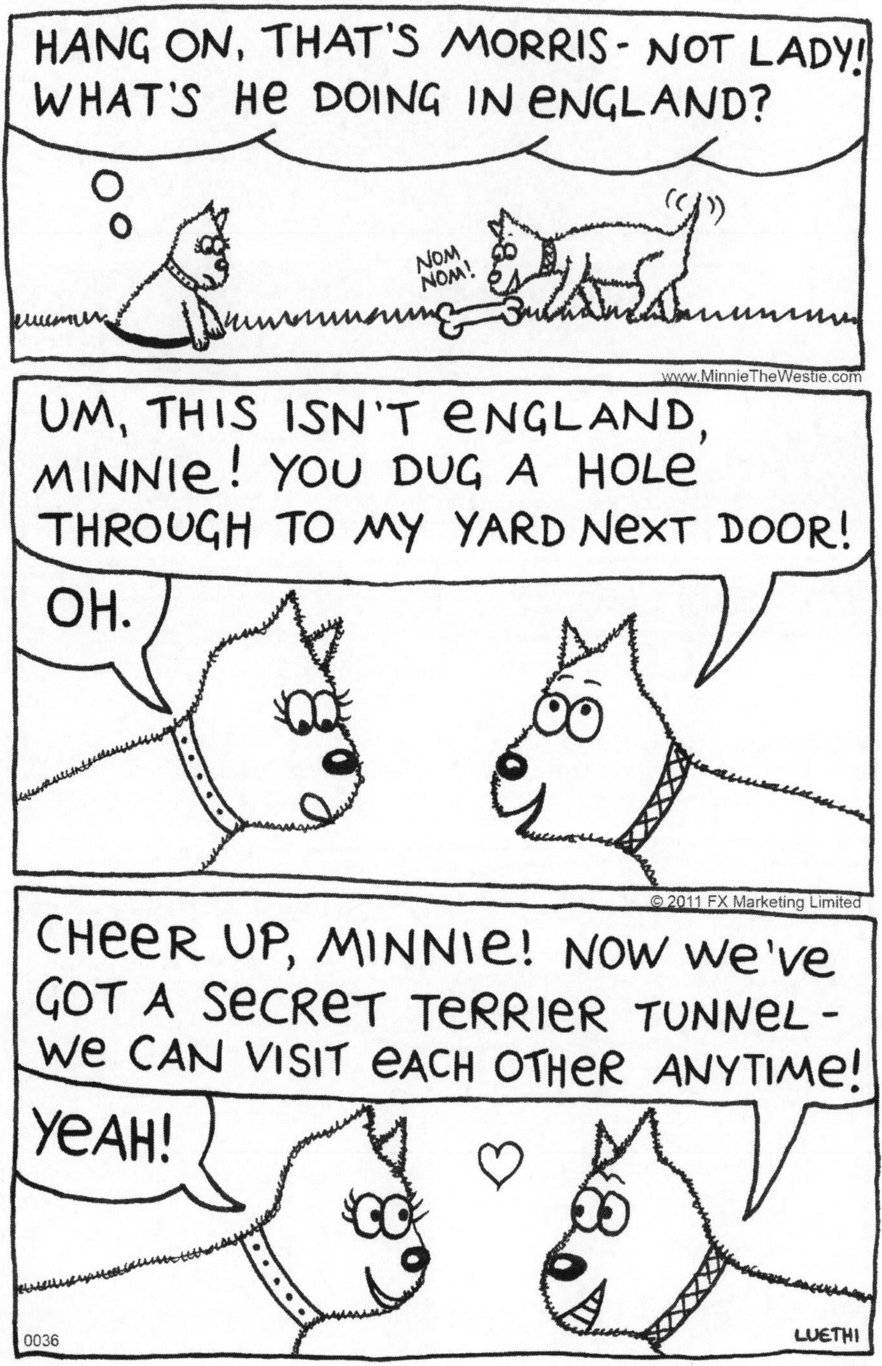
HANG ON, THAT'S MORRIS- NOT LADY! WHAT'S HE DOING IN ENGLAND?
NOM NOM!
www.MinnieTheWestie.com
UM, THIS ISN'T ENGLAND, MINNIE! YOU DUG A HOLE THROUGH TO MY YARD NEXT DOOR!
OH.
© 2011 FX Marketing Limited
CHEER UP, MINNIE! NOW WE'VE GOT A SECRET TERRIER TUNNEL - WE CAN VISIT EACH OTHER ANYTIME!
YEAH!
0036
LUETHI

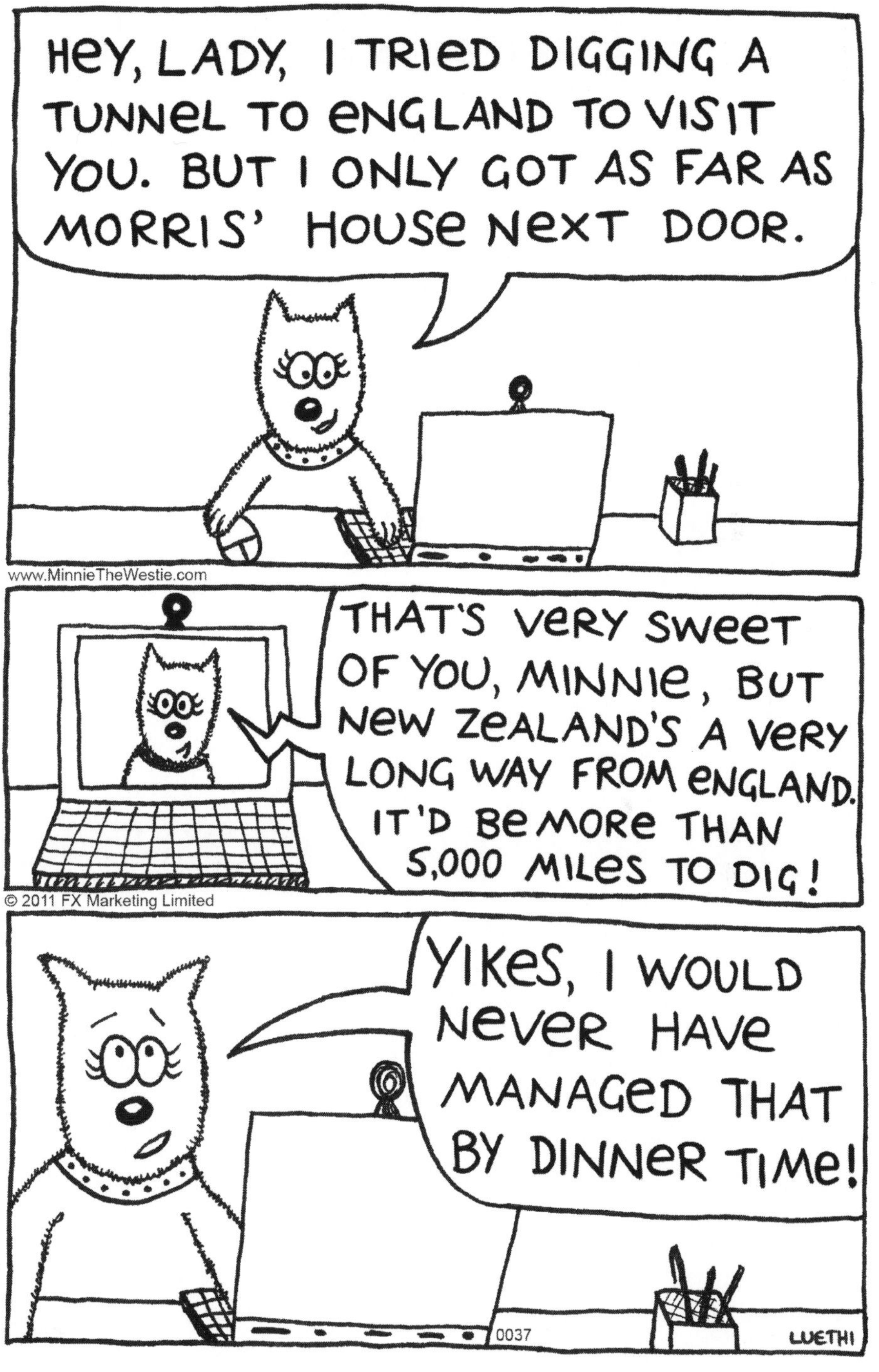
HEY, LADY, I TRIED DIGGING A TUNNEL TO ENGLAND TO VISIT YOU. BUT I ONLY GOT AS FAR AS MORRIS' HOUSE NEXT DOOR.
www.MinnieTheWestie.com
THAT'S VERY SWEET OF YOU, MINNIE, BUT NEW ZEALAND'S A VERY LONG WAY FROM ENGLAND. IT'D BE MORE THAN 5,000 MILES TO DIG!
© 2011 FX Marketing Limited
YIKES, I WOULD NEVER HAVE MANAGED THAT BY DINNER TIME!
0037
LUETHI

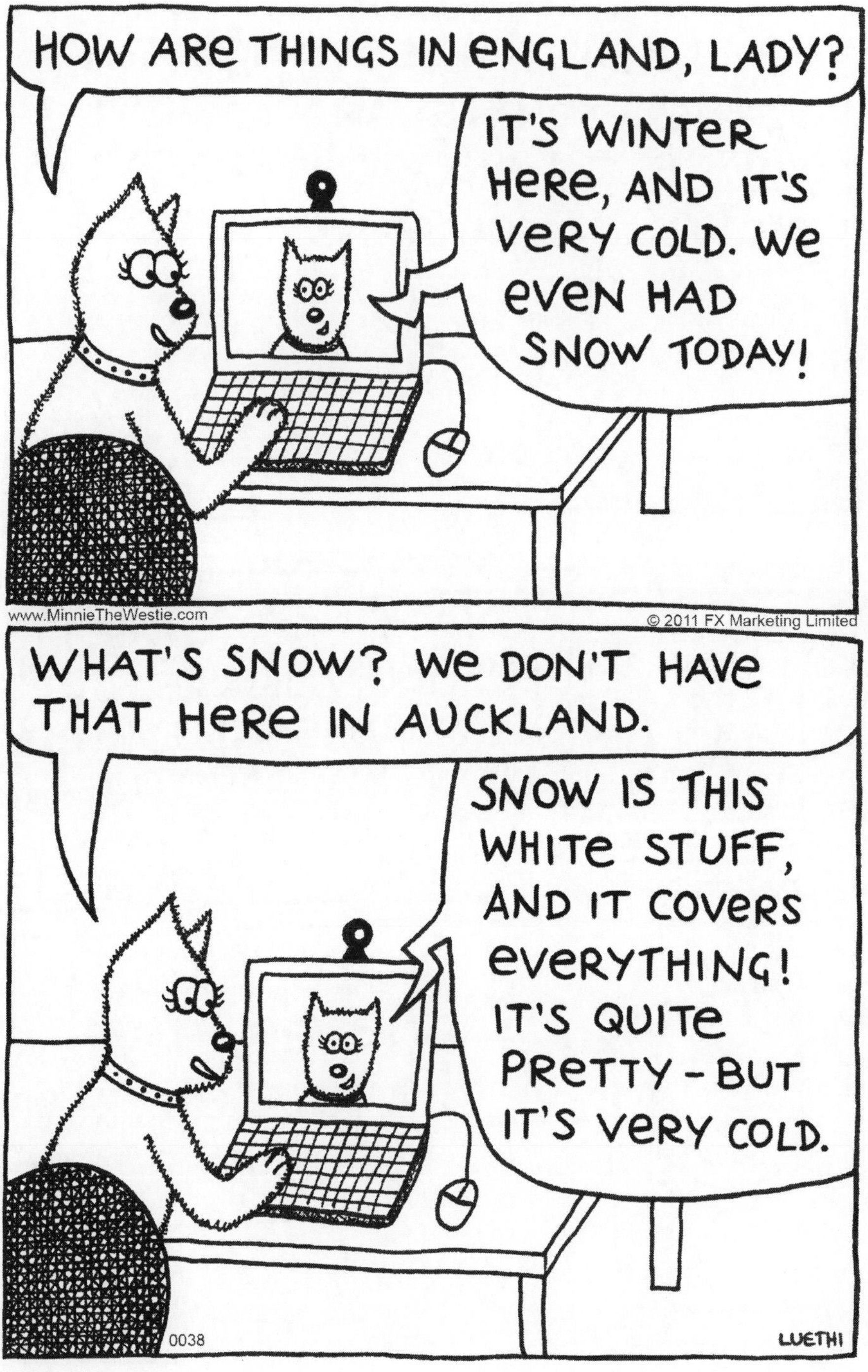
HOW ARE THINGS IN ENGLAND, LADY?
IT'S WINTER HERE, AND IT'S VERY COLD. WE EVEN HAD SNOW TODAY!
www.MinnieTheWestie.com
© 2011 FX Marketing Limited
WHAT'S SNOW? WE DON'T HAVE THAT HERE IN AUCKLAND.
SNOW IS THIS WHITE STUFF, AND IT COVERS EVERYTHING! IT'S QUITE PRETTY - BUT IT'S VERY COLD.
0038
LUETHI

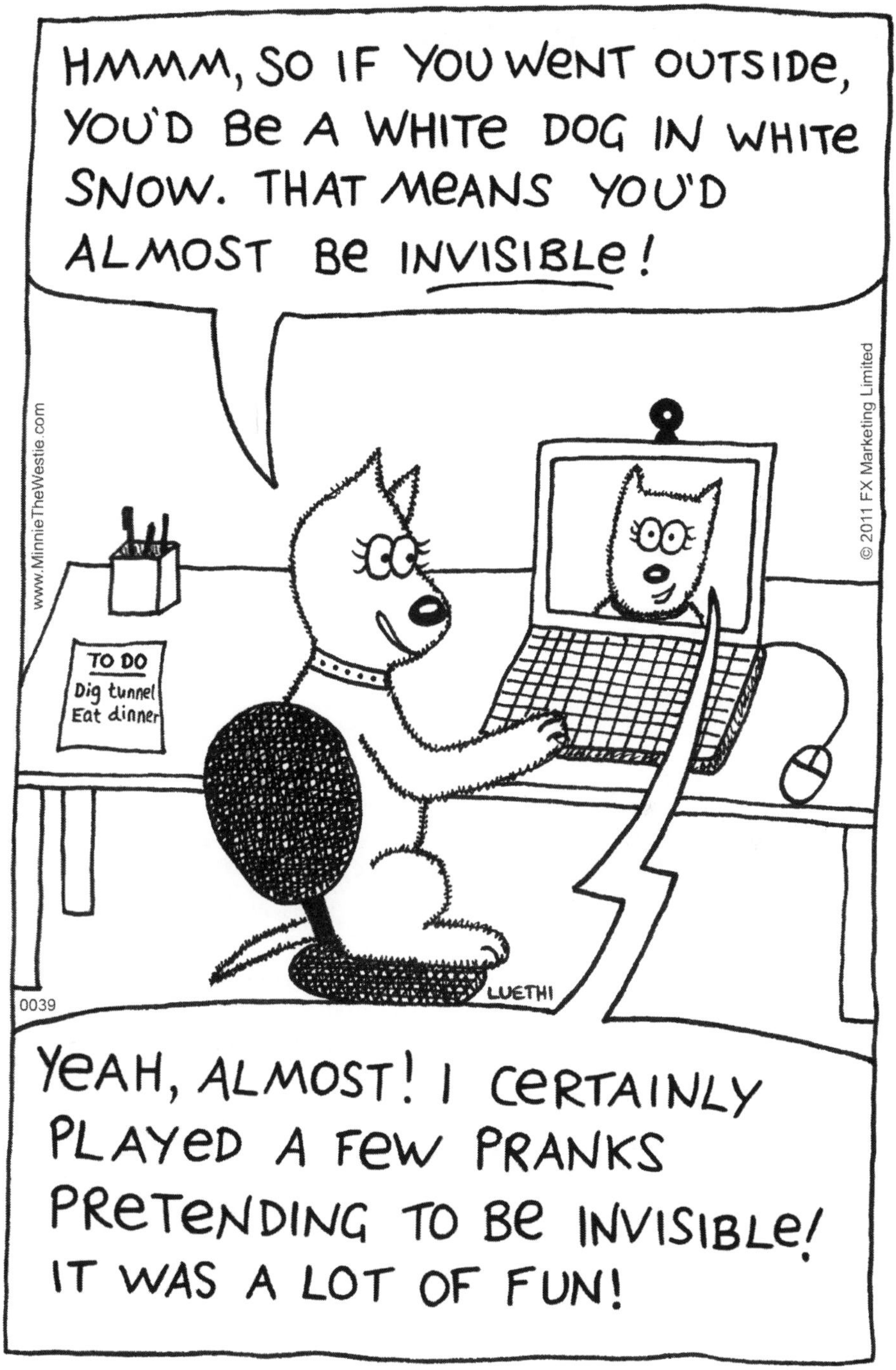
HMMM, SO IF YOU WENT OUTSIDE, YOU'D BE A WHITE DOG IN WHITE SNOW. THAT MEANS YOU'D ALMOST BE INVISIBLE!
TO DO
Dig tunnel
Eat dinner
YEAH, ALMOST! I CERTAINLY PLAYED A FEW PRANKS PRETENDING TO BE INVISIBLE! IT WAS A LOT OF FUN!
LUETHI
www.MinnieTheWestie.com
© 2011 FX Marketing Limited
0039

LADY WAS TELLING ME ABOUT THIS WHITE STUFF CALLED 'SNOW'. IT ALMOST MADE HER INVISIBLE!
COOL!
www.MinnieTheWestie.com
I WANT TO BE INVISIBLE FOR A WHILE, TOO. WE NEED TO FIND SOMETHING WHITE...
© 2011 FX Marketing Limited
HOW ABOUT YOUR PILLOWCASE?
PERFECT!
0040
LUETHI

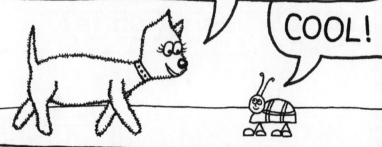

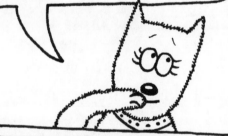

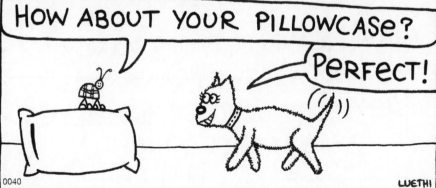

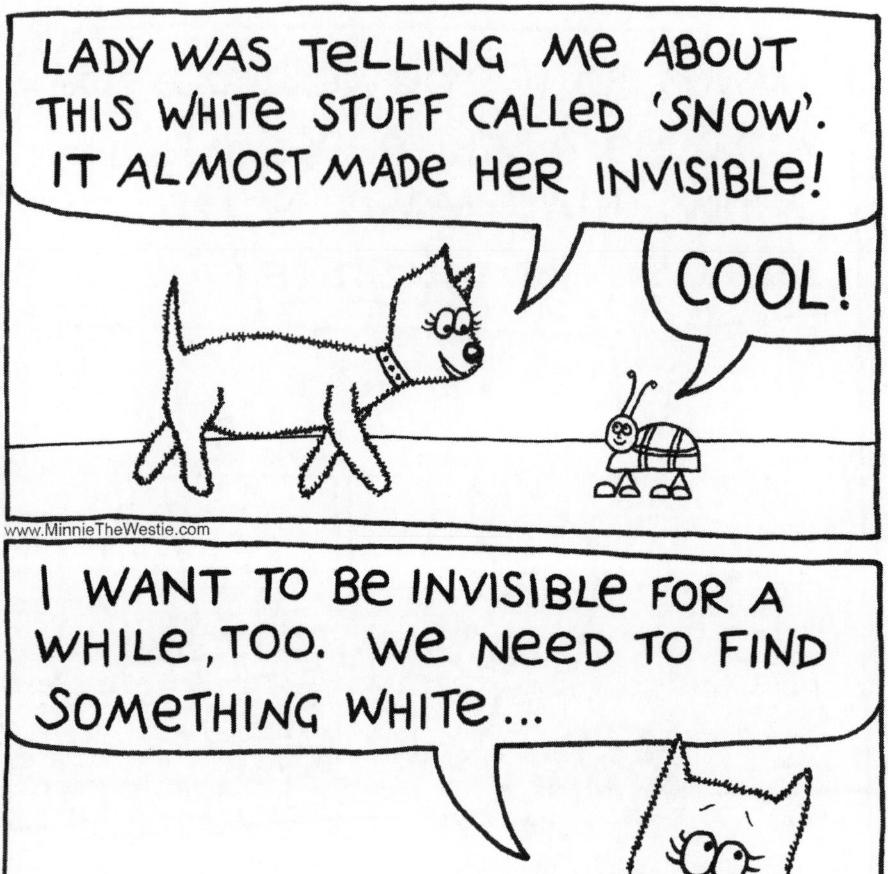

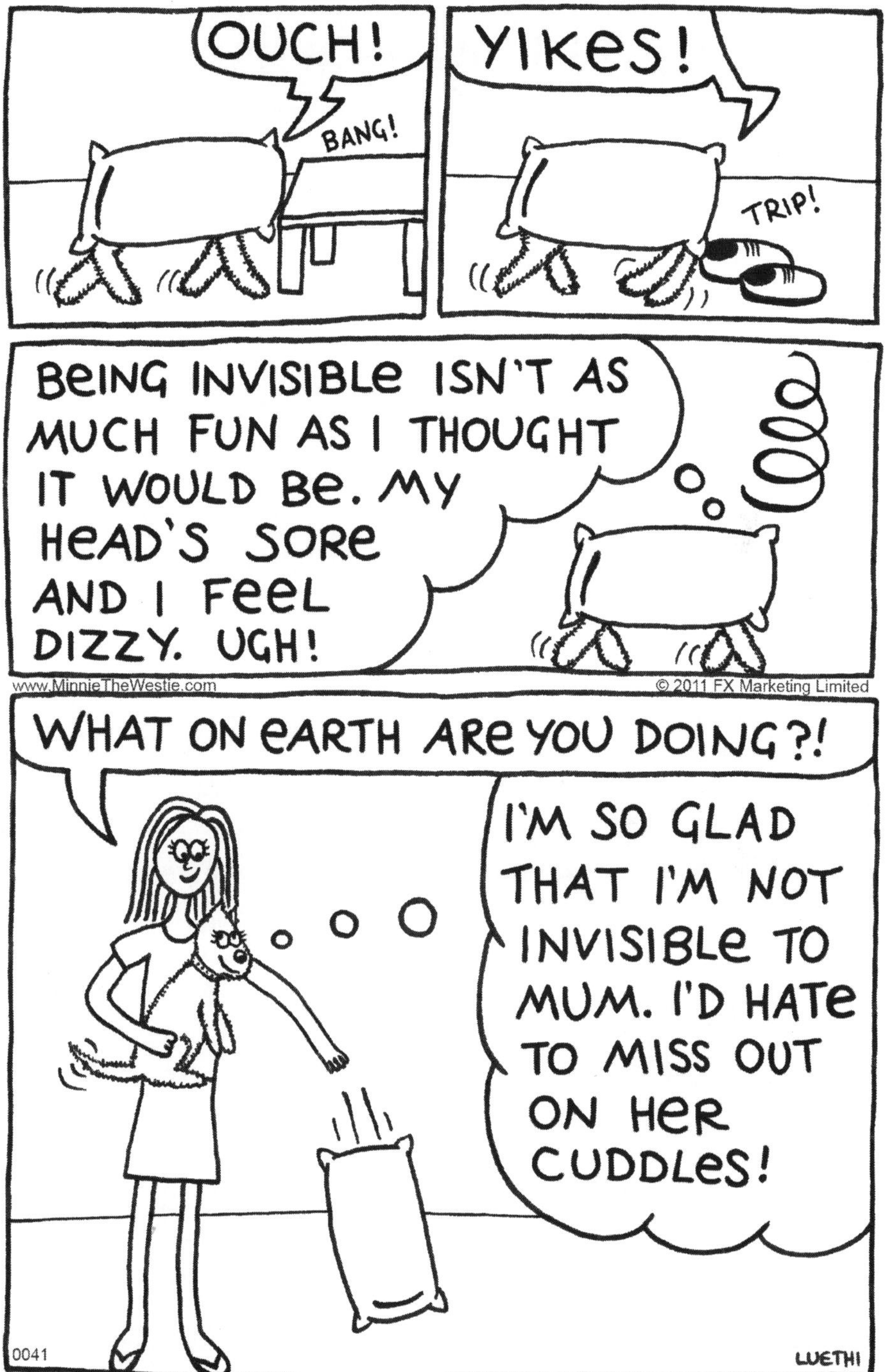
OUCH!
BANG!
YIKES!
TRIP!
BEING INVISIBLE ISN'T AS MUCH FUN AS I THOUGHT IT WOULD BE. MY HEAD'S SORE AND I FEEL DIZZY. UGH!
www.MinnieTheWestie.com
© 2011 FX Marketing Limited
WHAT ON EARTH ARE YOU DOING?!
I'M SO GLAD THAT I'M NOT INVISIBLE TO MUM. I'D HATE TO MISS OUT ON HER CUDDLES!
0041
LUETHI

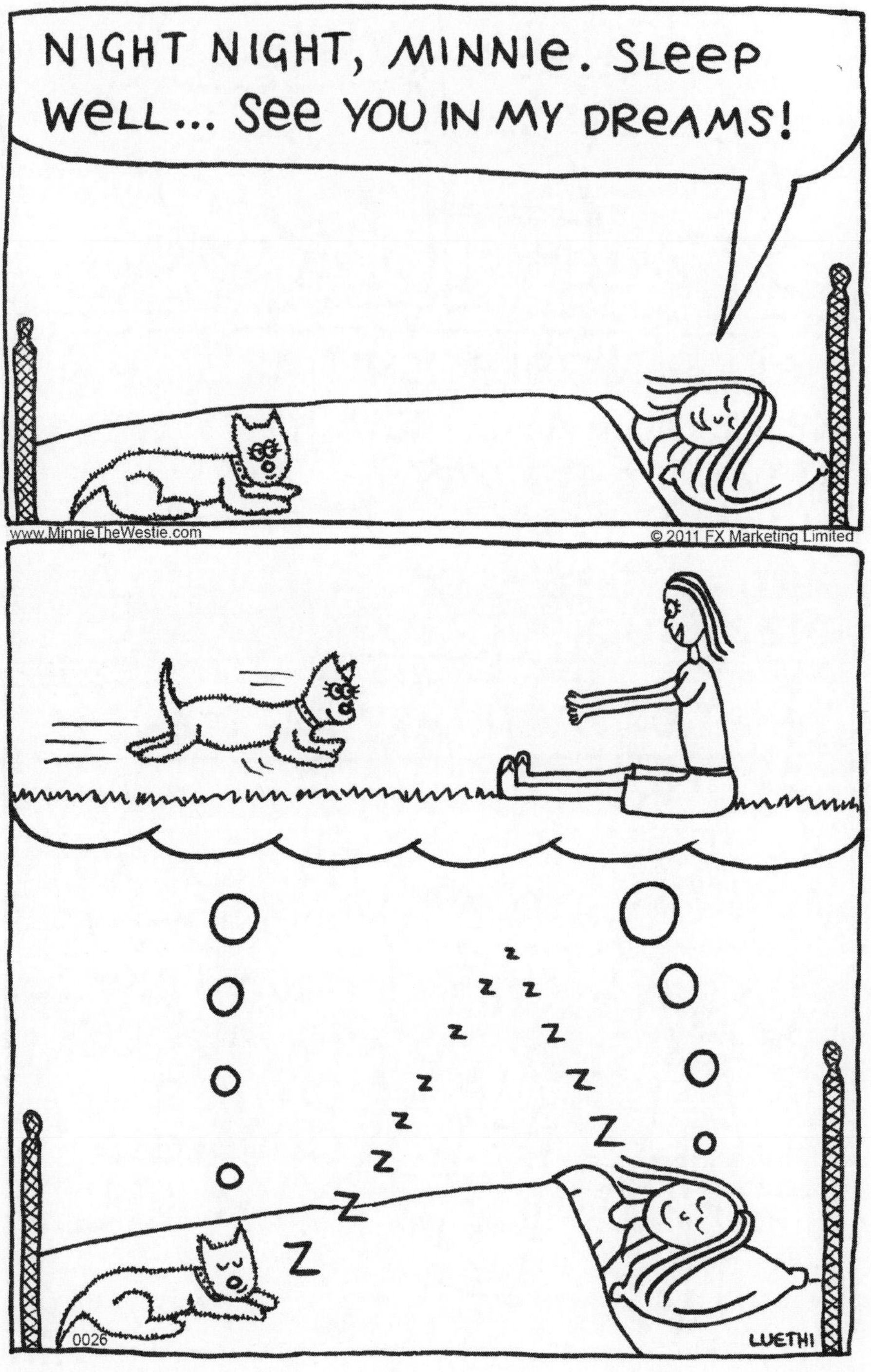
NIGHT NIGHT, MINNIE. SLEEP WELL... SEE YOU IN MY DREAMS!
www.MinnieTheWestie.com
© 2011 FX Marketing Limited
Z Z Z Z Z Z Z Z Z Z Z
0026
LUETHI

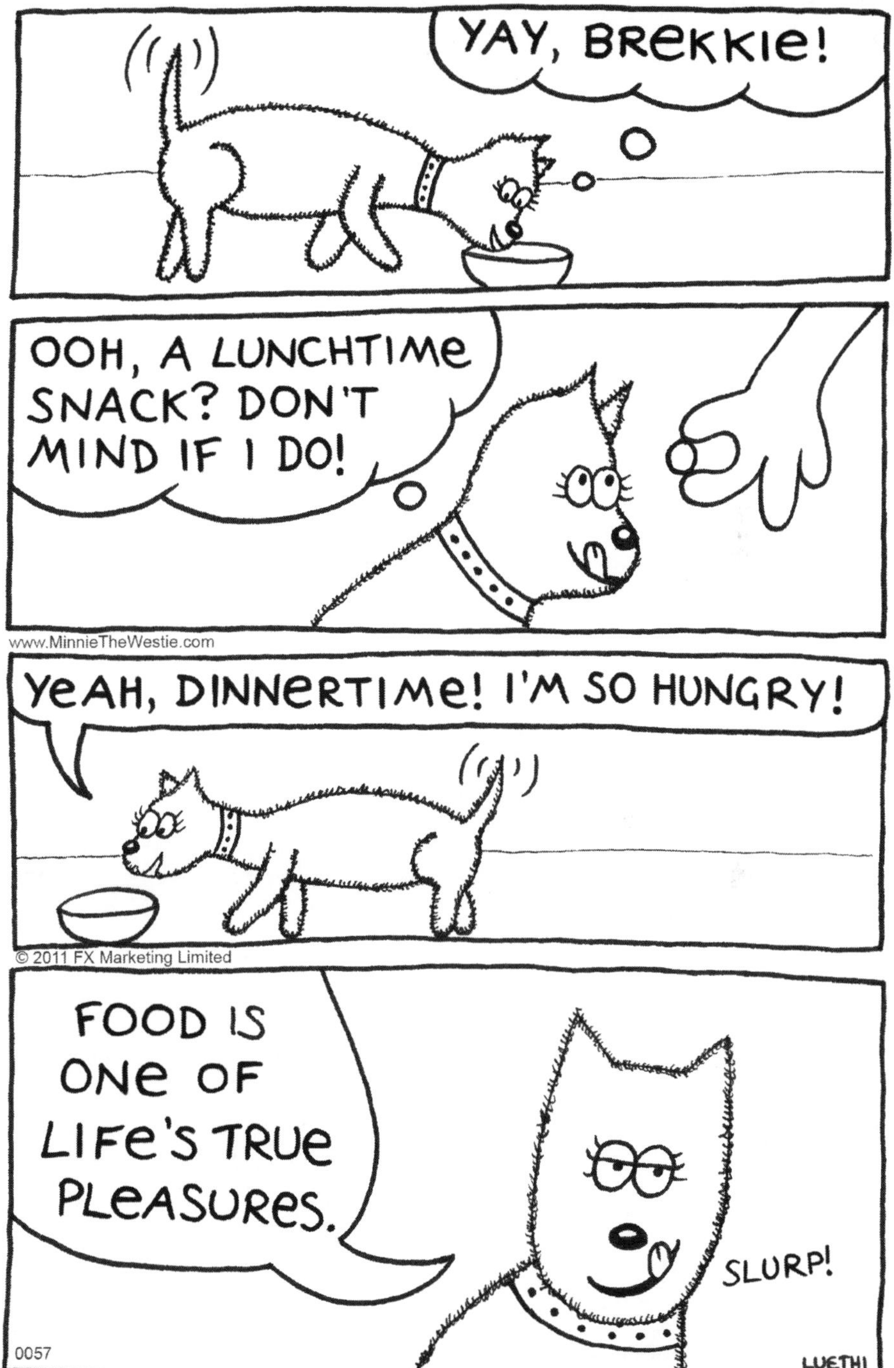
YAY, BREKKIE!
OOH, A LUNCHTIME SNACK? DON'T MIND IF I DO!
www.MinnieTheWestie.com
YEAH, DINNERTIME! I'M SO HUNGRY!
© 2011 FX Marketing Limited
FOOD IS ONE OF LIFE'S TRUE PLEASURES.
SLURP!
0057
LUETHI

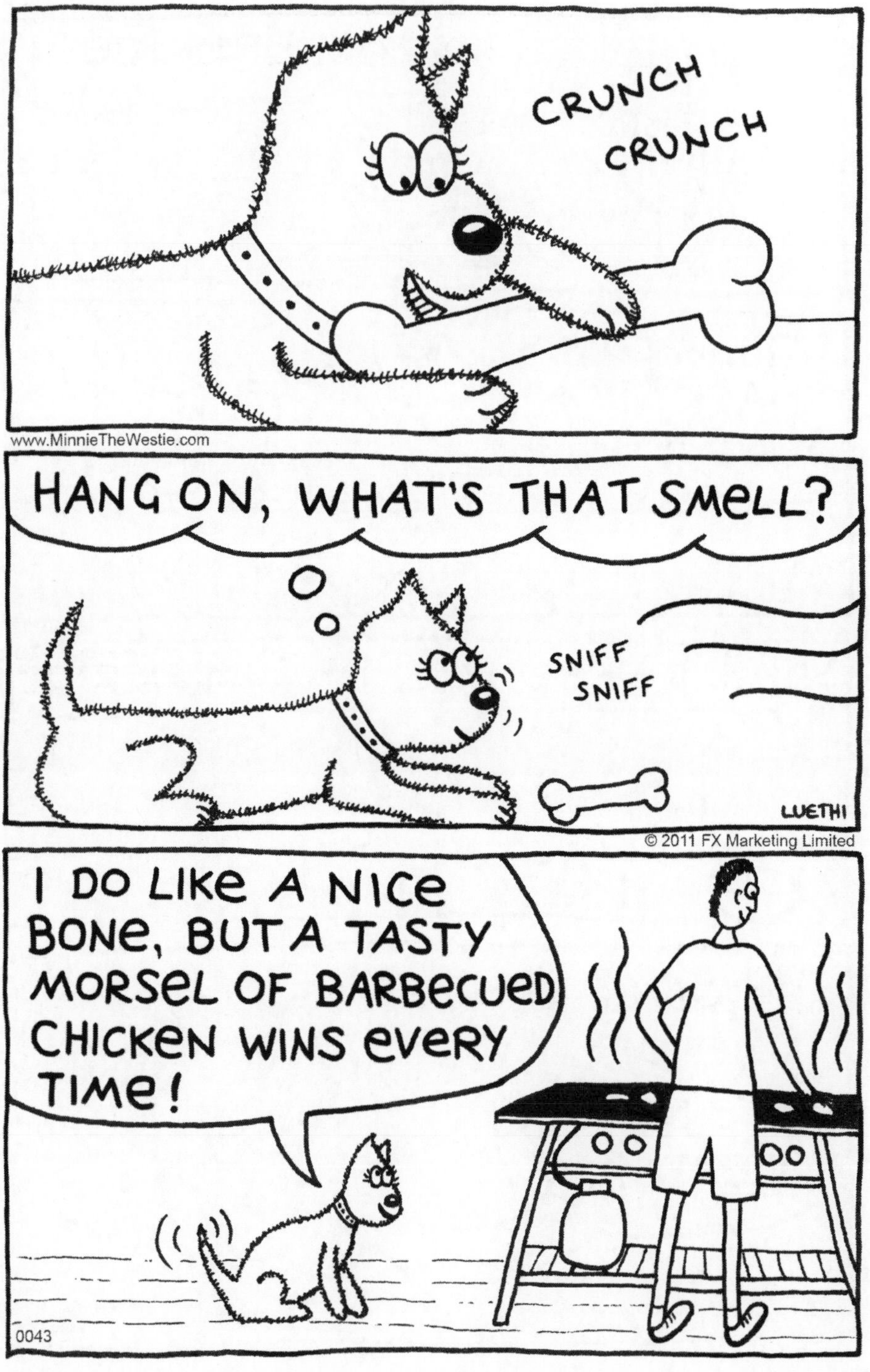
CRUNCH
CRUNCH
HANG ON, WHAT'S THAT SMELL?
SNIFF
SNIFF
LUETHI
I DO LIKE A NICE BONE, BUT A TASTY MORSEL OF BARBECUED CHICKEN WINS EVERY TIME!
0043

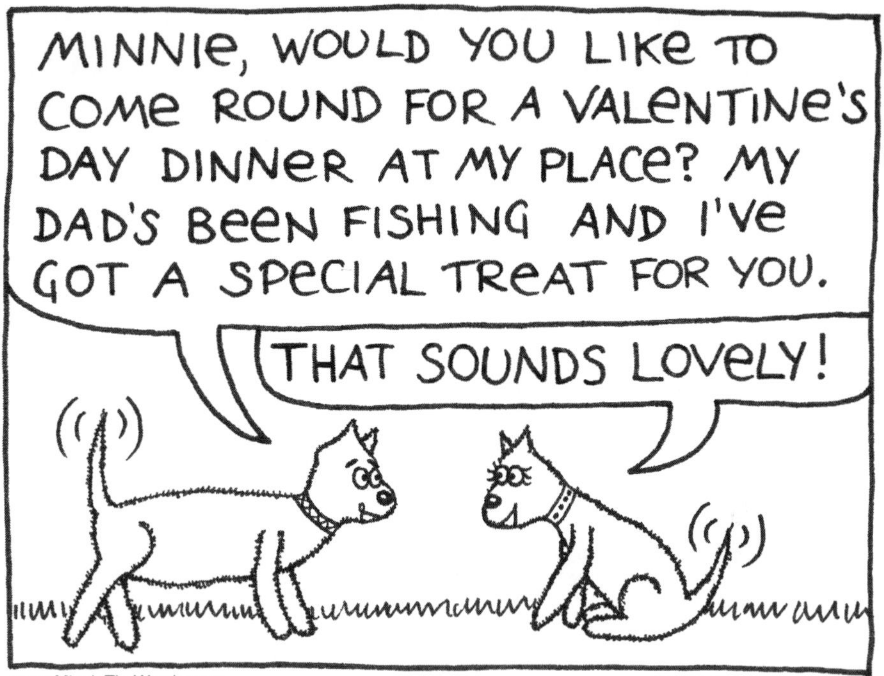
MINNIE, WOULD YOU LIKE TO COME ROUND FOR A VALENTINE'S DAY DINNER AT MY PLACE? MY DAD'S BEEN FISHING AND I'VE GOT A SPECIAL TREAT FOR YOU.
THAT SOUNDS LOVELY!

www.MinnieTheWestie.com

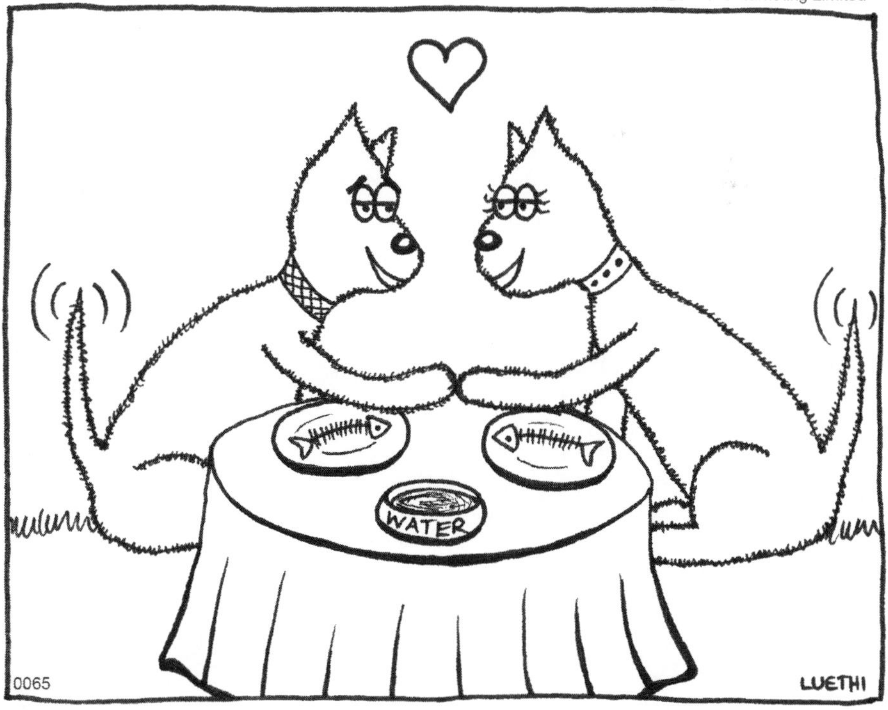
WATER
0065
LUETHI

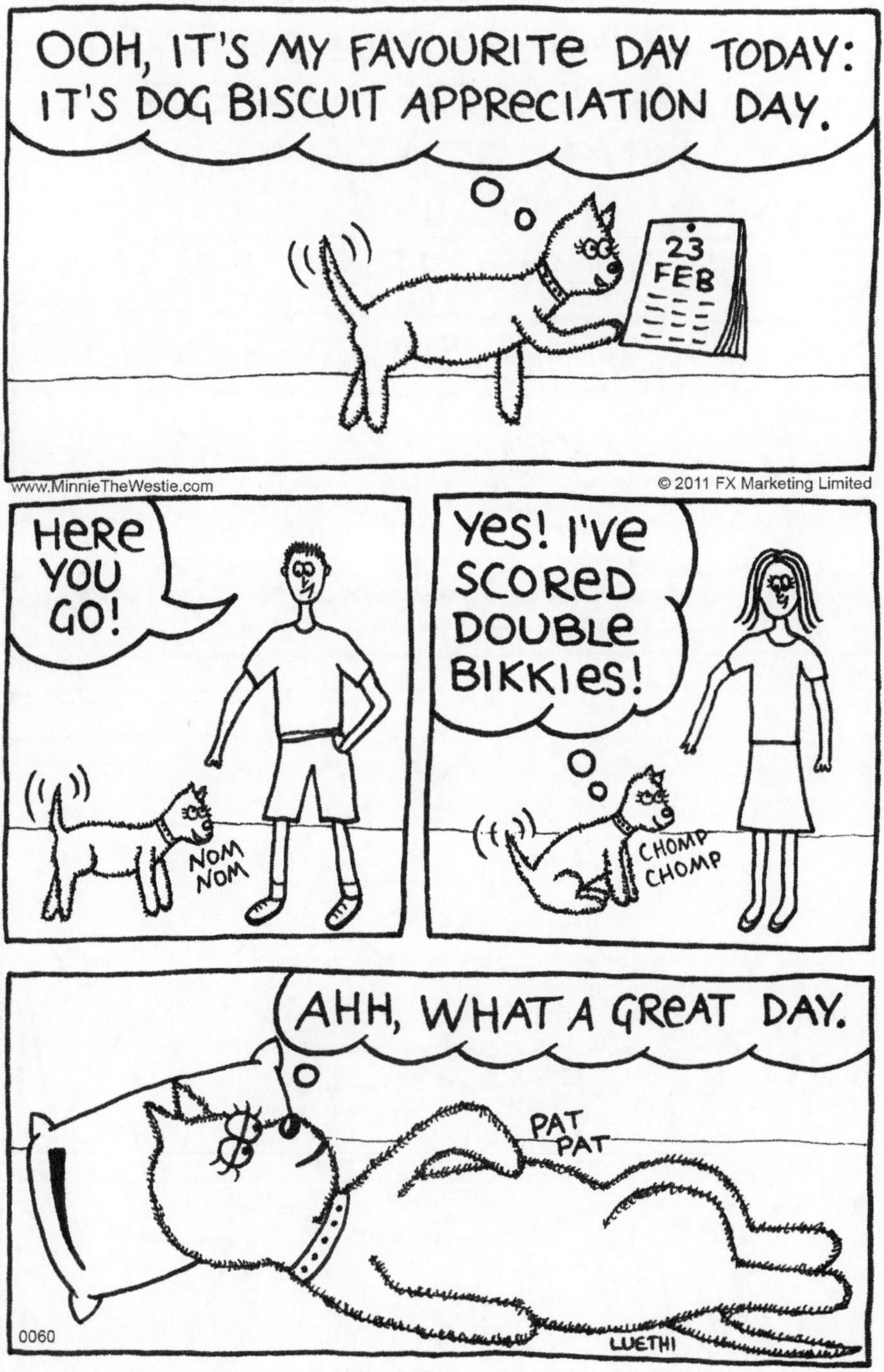
OOH, IT'S MY FAVOURITE DAY TODAY: IT'S DOG BISCUIT APPRECIATION DAY.
23 FEB
www.MinnieTheWestie.com
© 2011 FX Marketing Limited
HERE YOU GO!
NOM NOM
YES! I'VE SCORED DOUBLE BIKKIES!
CHOMP CHOMP
AHH, WHAT A GREAT DAY.
PAT PAT
0060
LUETHI

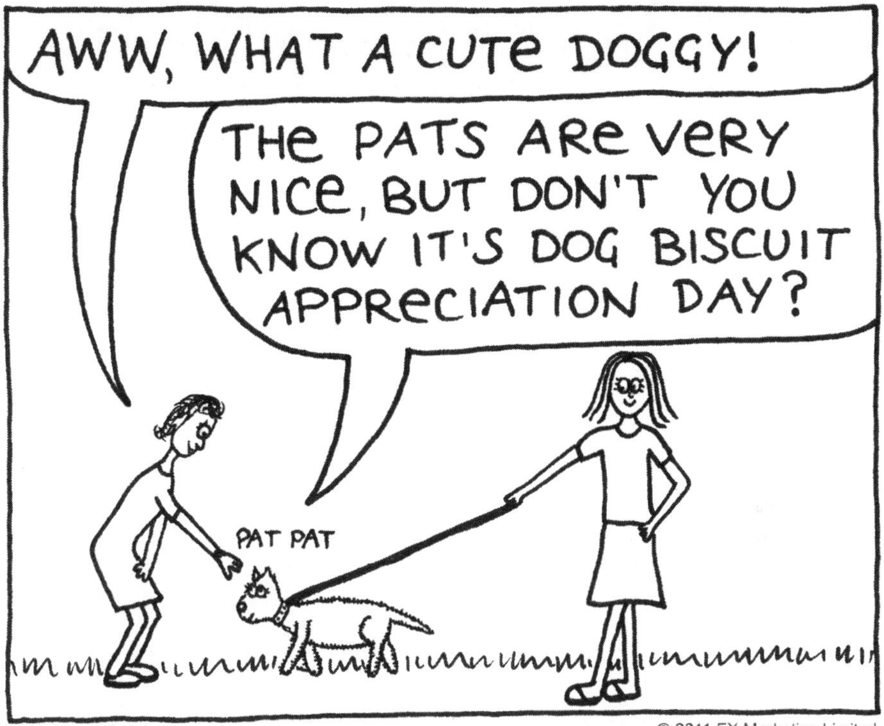
AWW, WHAT A CUTE DOGGY!
THE PATS ARE VERY NICE, BUT DON'T YOU KNOW IT'S DOG BISCUIT APPRECIATION DAY?
PAT PAT

www.MinnieTheWestie.com

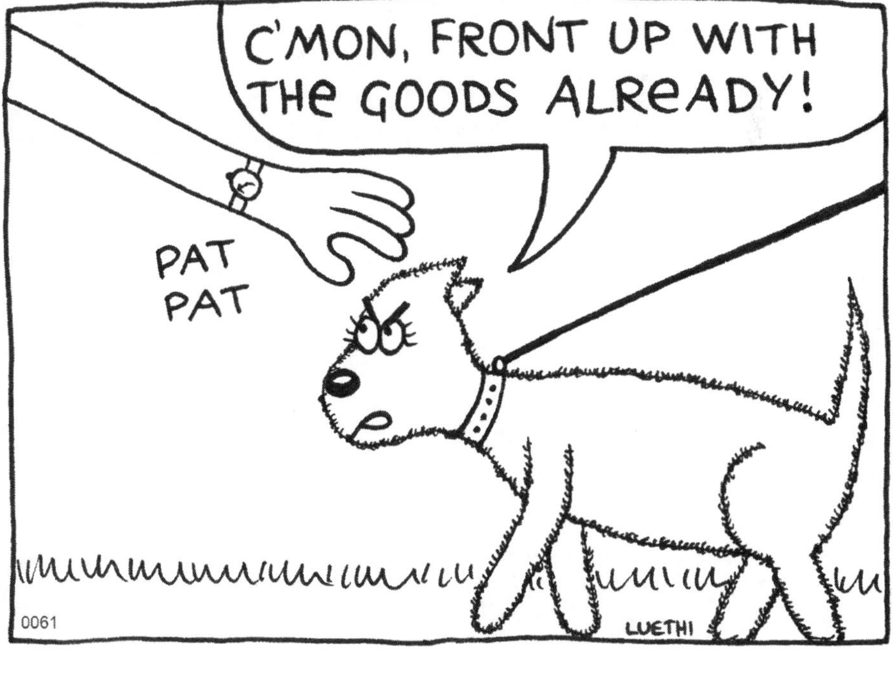
C'MON, FRONT UP WITH THE GOODS ALREADY!
PAT PAT
0061
LUETHI

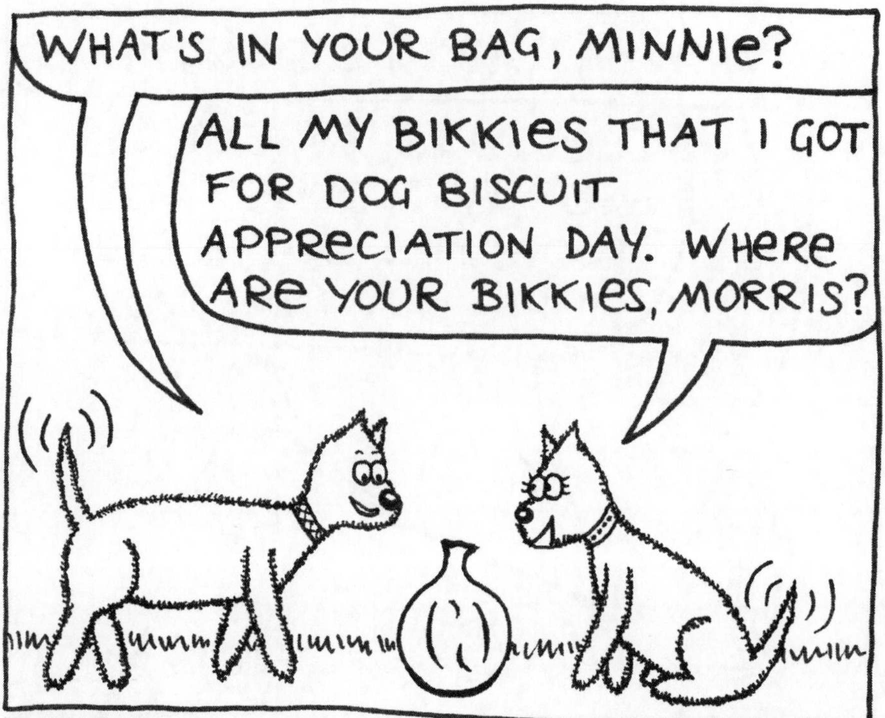
WHAT'S IN YOUR BAG, MINNIE?
ALL MY BIKKIES THAT I GOT FOR DOG BISCUIT APPRECIATION DAY. WHERE ARE YOUR BIKKIES, MORRIS?

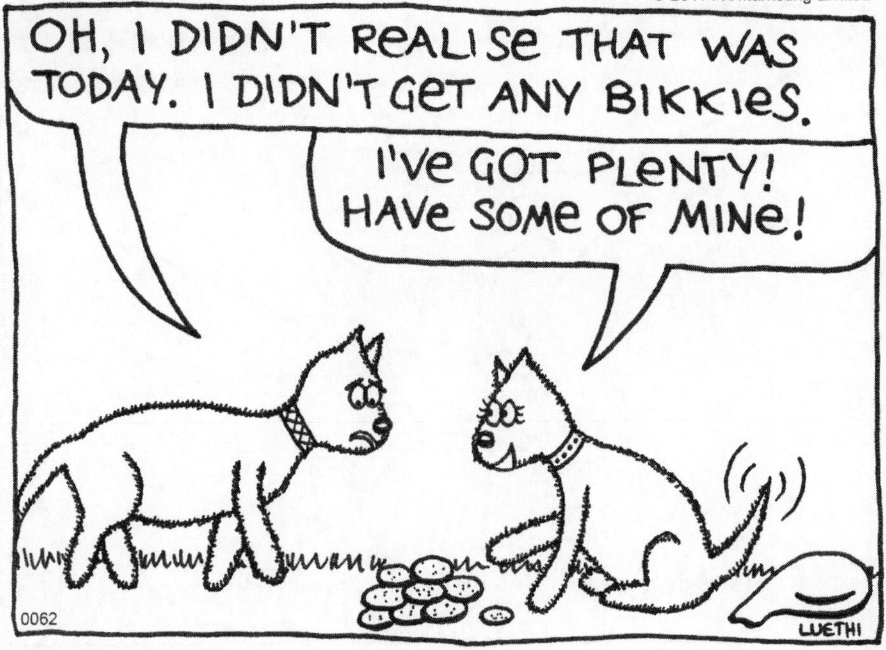
OH, I DIDN'T REALISE THAT WAS TODAY. I DIDN'T GET ANY BIKKIES.
I'VE GOT PLENTY! HAVE SOME OF MINE!
0062
LUETHI

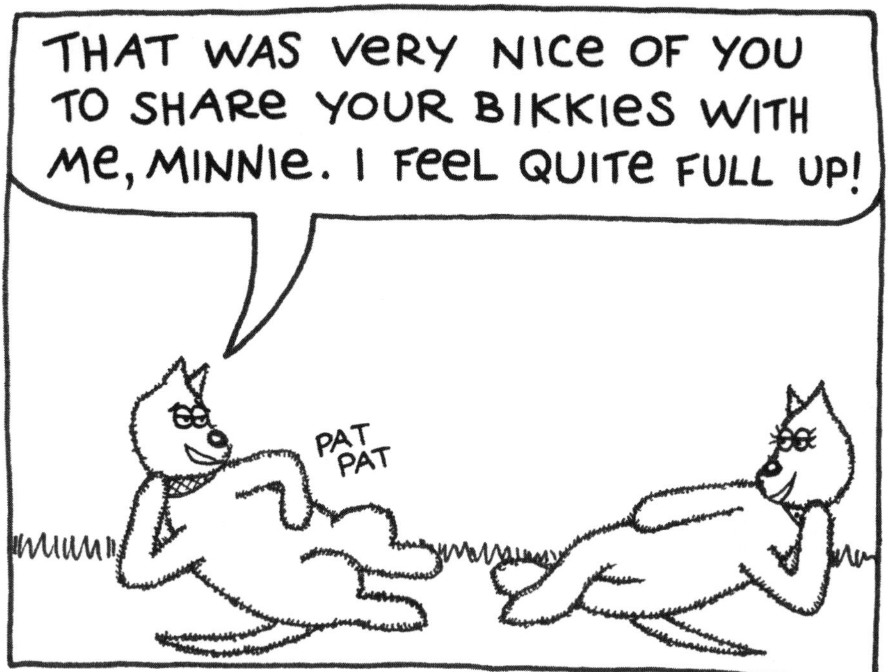
THAT WAS VERY NICE OF YOU TO SHARE YOUR BIKKIES WITH ME, MINNIE. I FEEL QUITE FULL UP!
PAT PAT

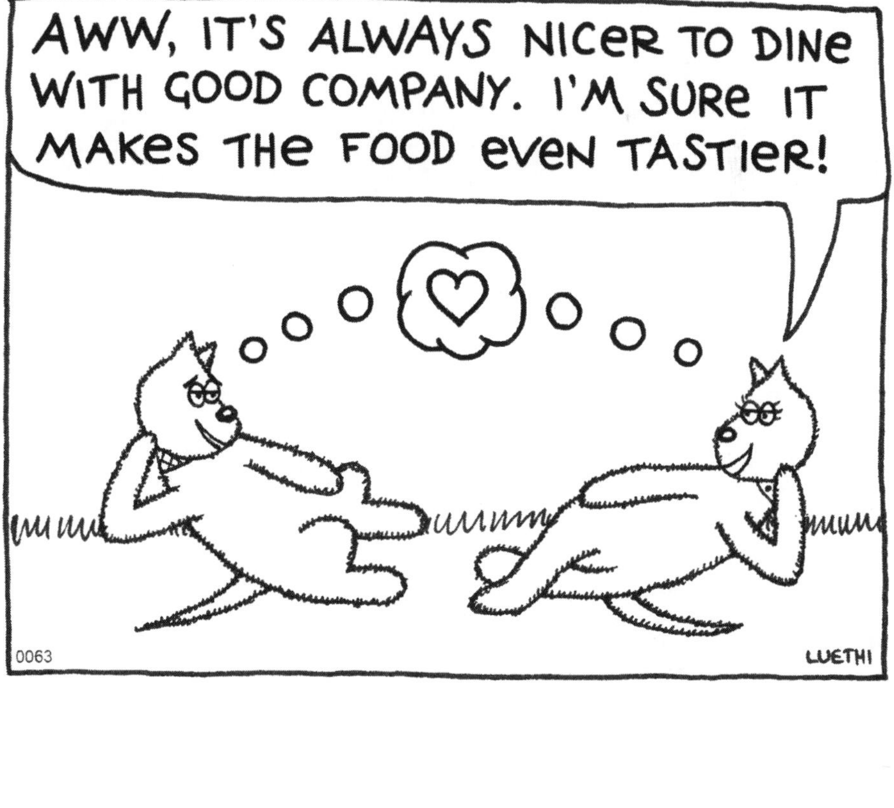
AWW, IT'S ALWAYS NICER TO DINE WITH GOOD COMPANY. I'M SURE IT MAKES THE FOOD EVEN TASTIER!
0063
LUETHI

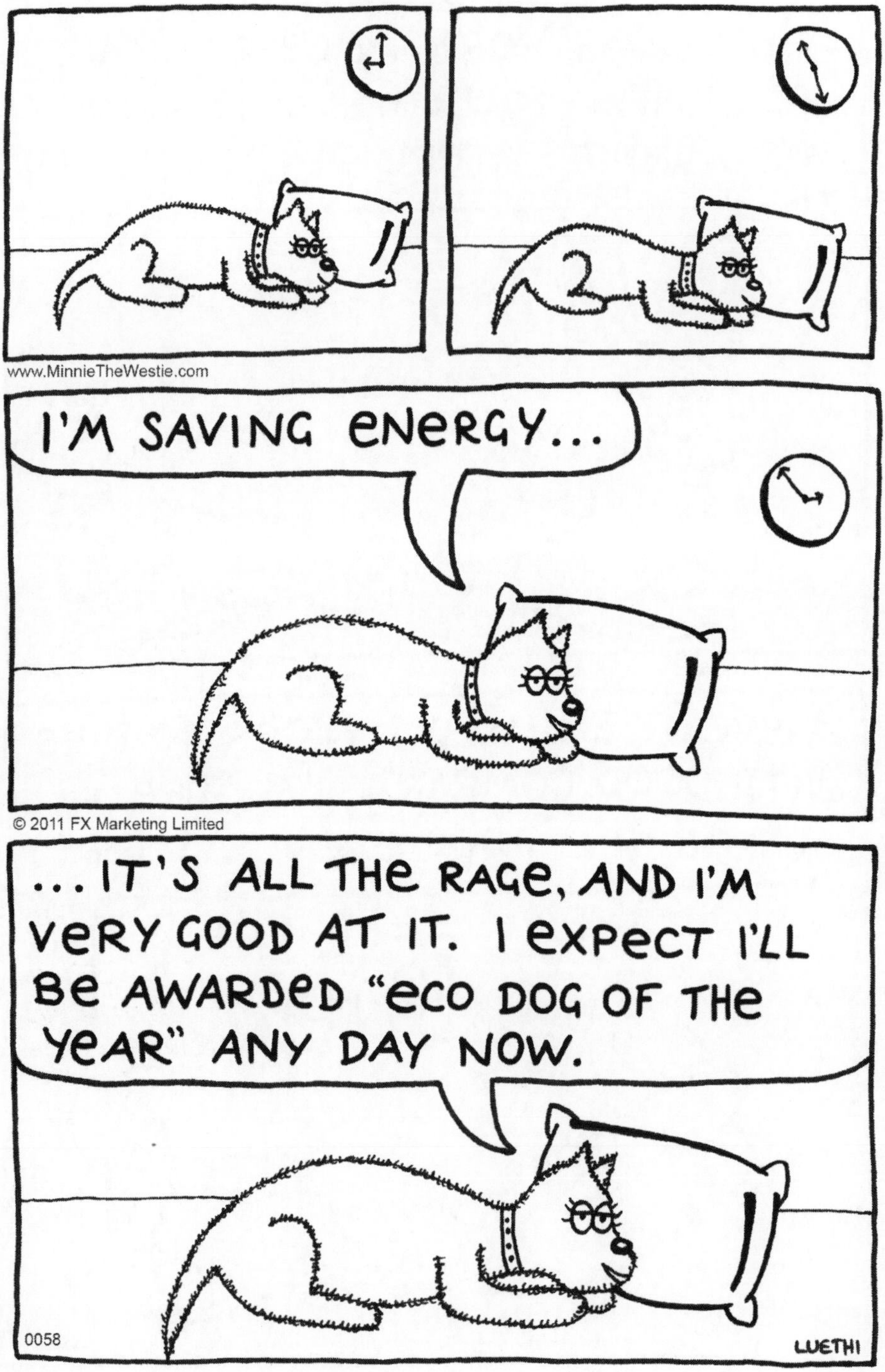
www.MinnieTheWestie.com
I'M SAVING ENERGY...
© 2011 FX Marketing Limited
...IT'S ALL THE RAGE, AND I'M VERY GOOD AT IT. I EXPECT I'LL BE AWARDED "ECO DOG OF THE YEAR" ANY DAY NOW.
0058
LUETHI

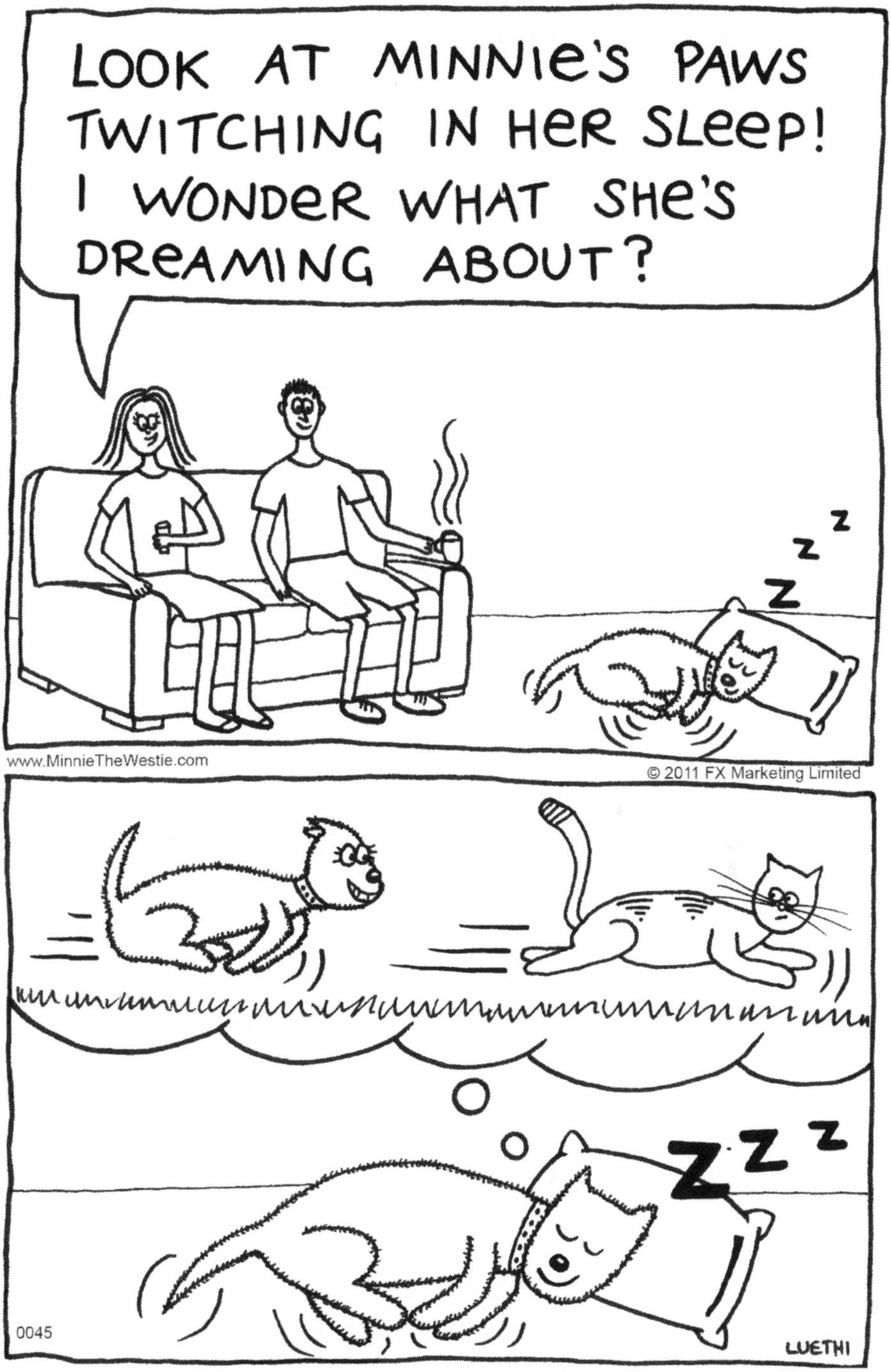
LOOK AT MINNIE'S PAWS TWITCHING IN HER SLEEP! I WONDER WHAT SHE'S DREAMING ABOUT?
Z Z Z
Z Z Z
0045
LUETHI

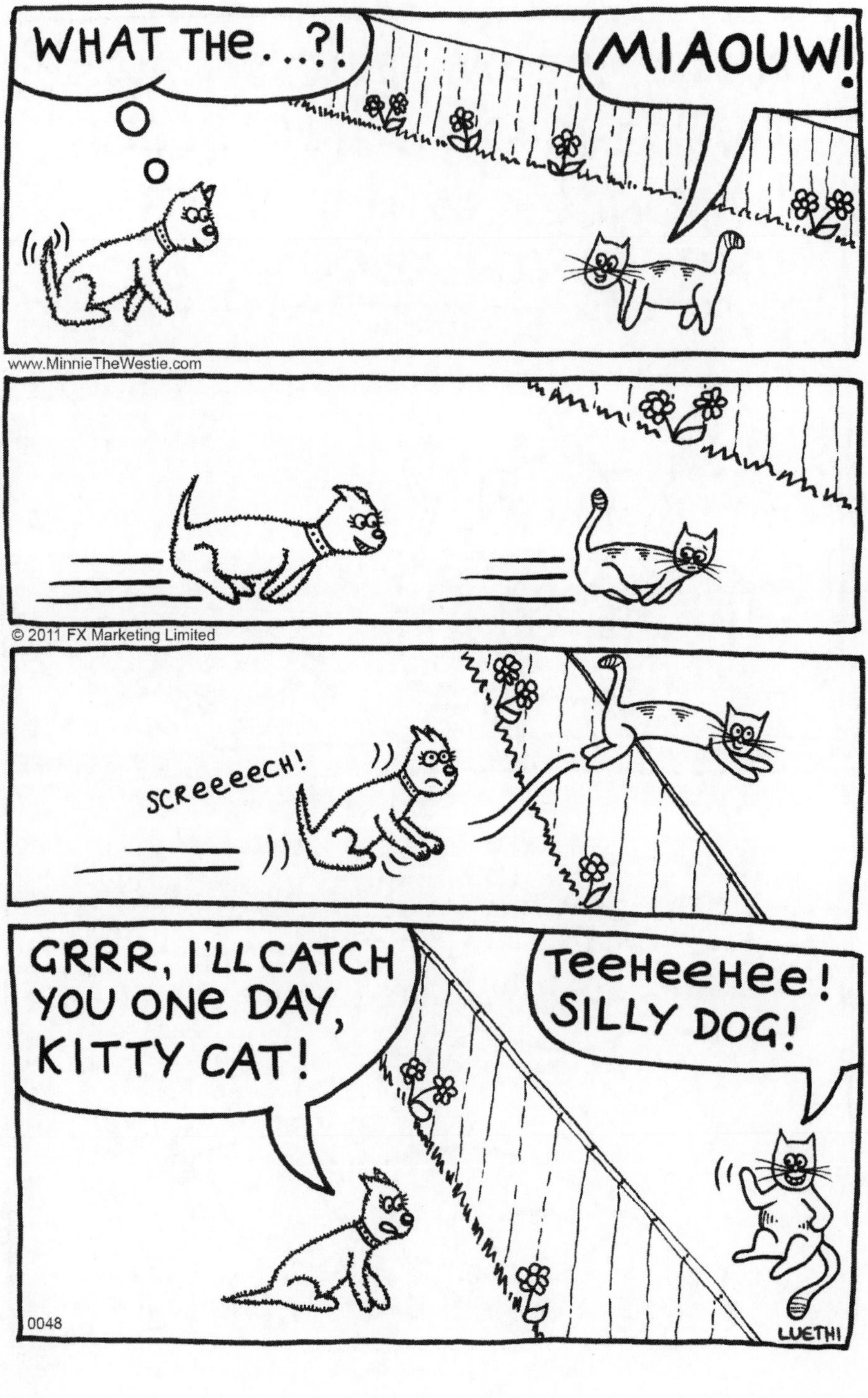
WHAT THE...?!
MIAOUW!
SCREEEECH!
GRRR, I'LL CATCH YOU ONE DAY, KITTY CAT!
TEEHEEHEE! SILLY DOG!
0048
LUETHI

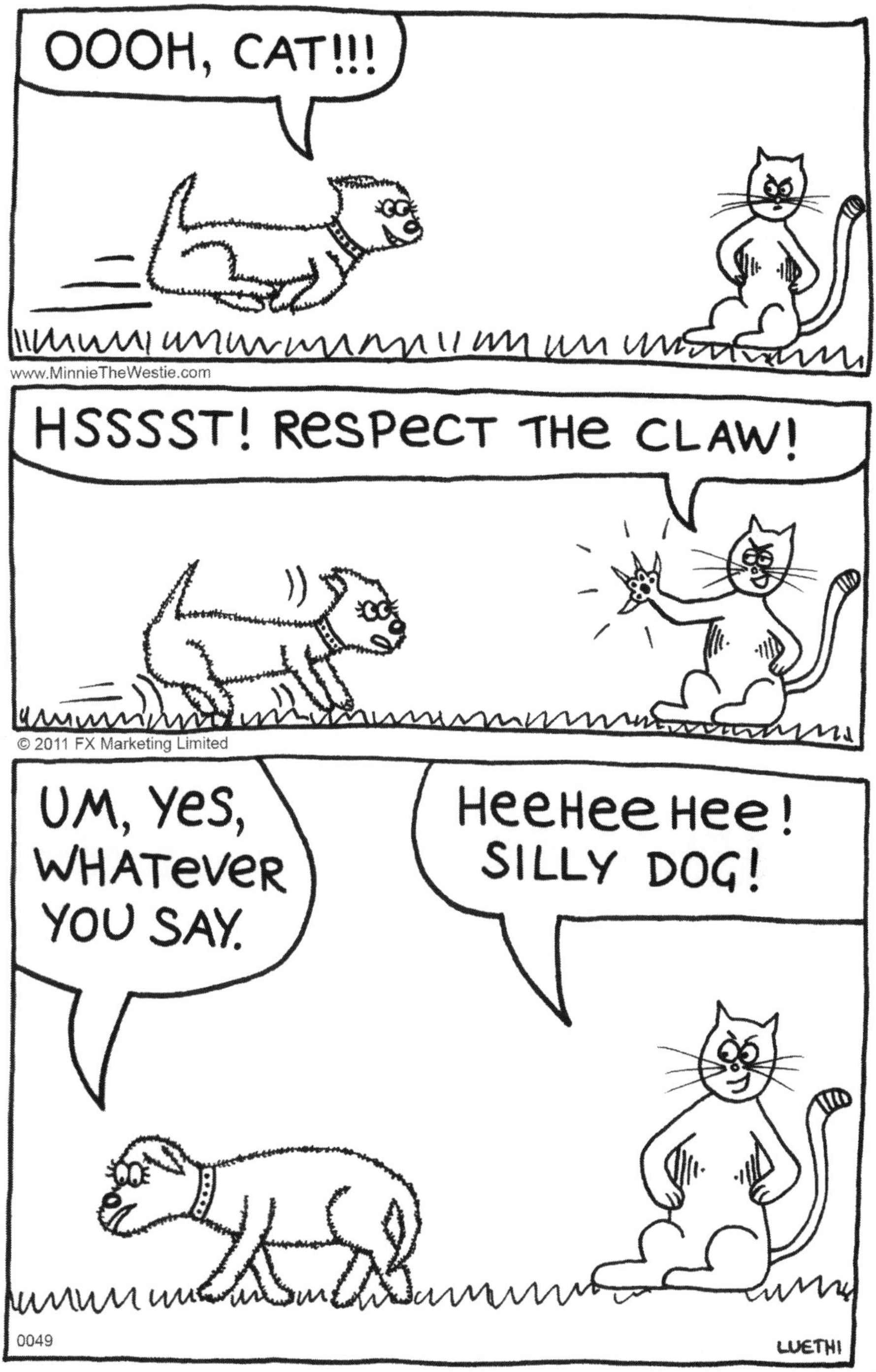
OOOH, CAT!!!
www.MinnieTheWestie.com
HSSSST! RESPECT THE CLAW!
UM, YES, WHATEVER YOU SAY.
HEEHEEHEE! SILLY DOG!
0049
LUETHI

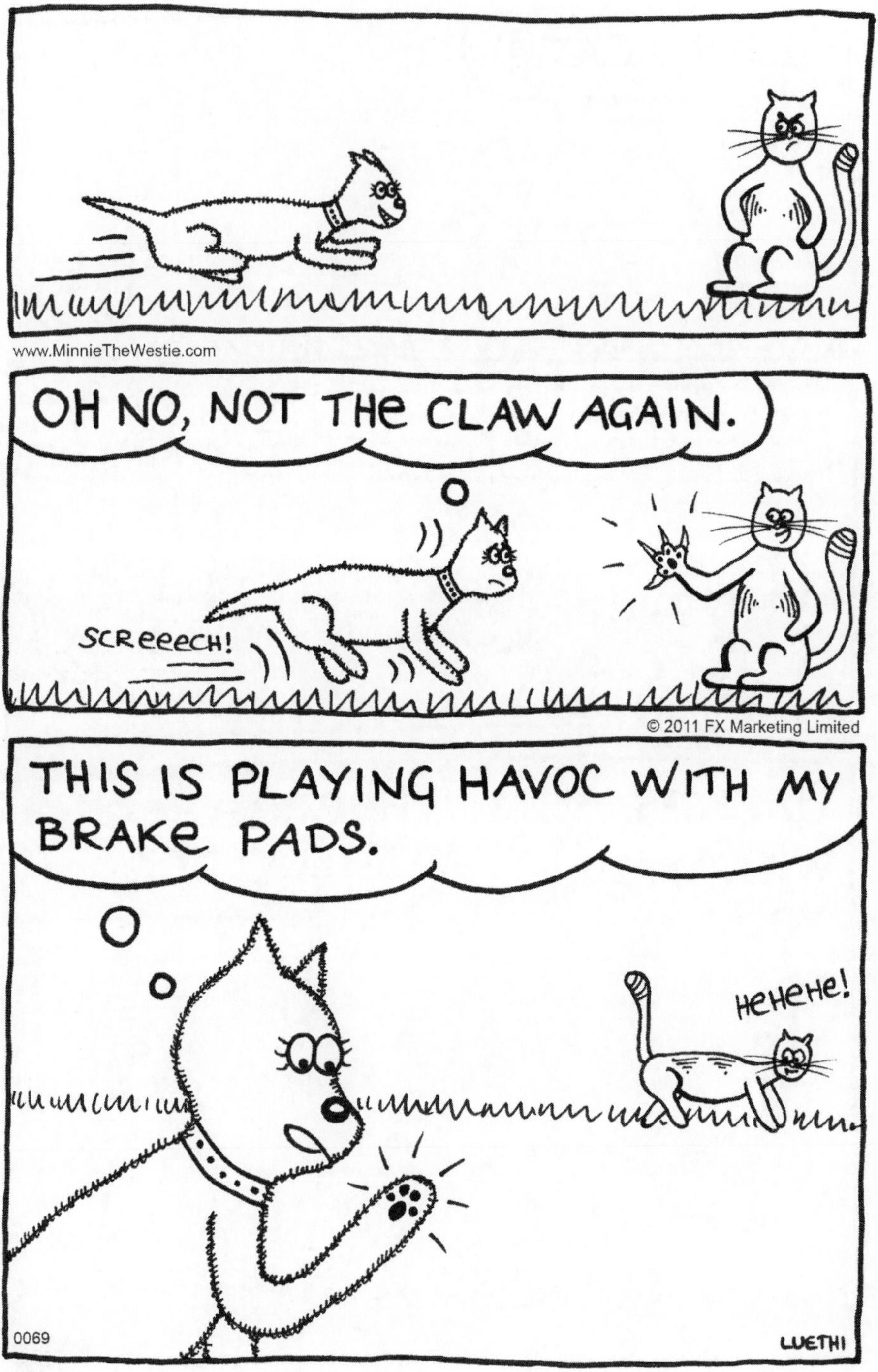
www.MinnieTheWestie.com
OH NO, NOT THE CLAW AGAIN.
SCREEECH!
© 2011 FX Marketing Limited
THIS IS PLAYING HAVOC WITH MY BRAKE PADS.
HEHEHE!
0069
LUETHI

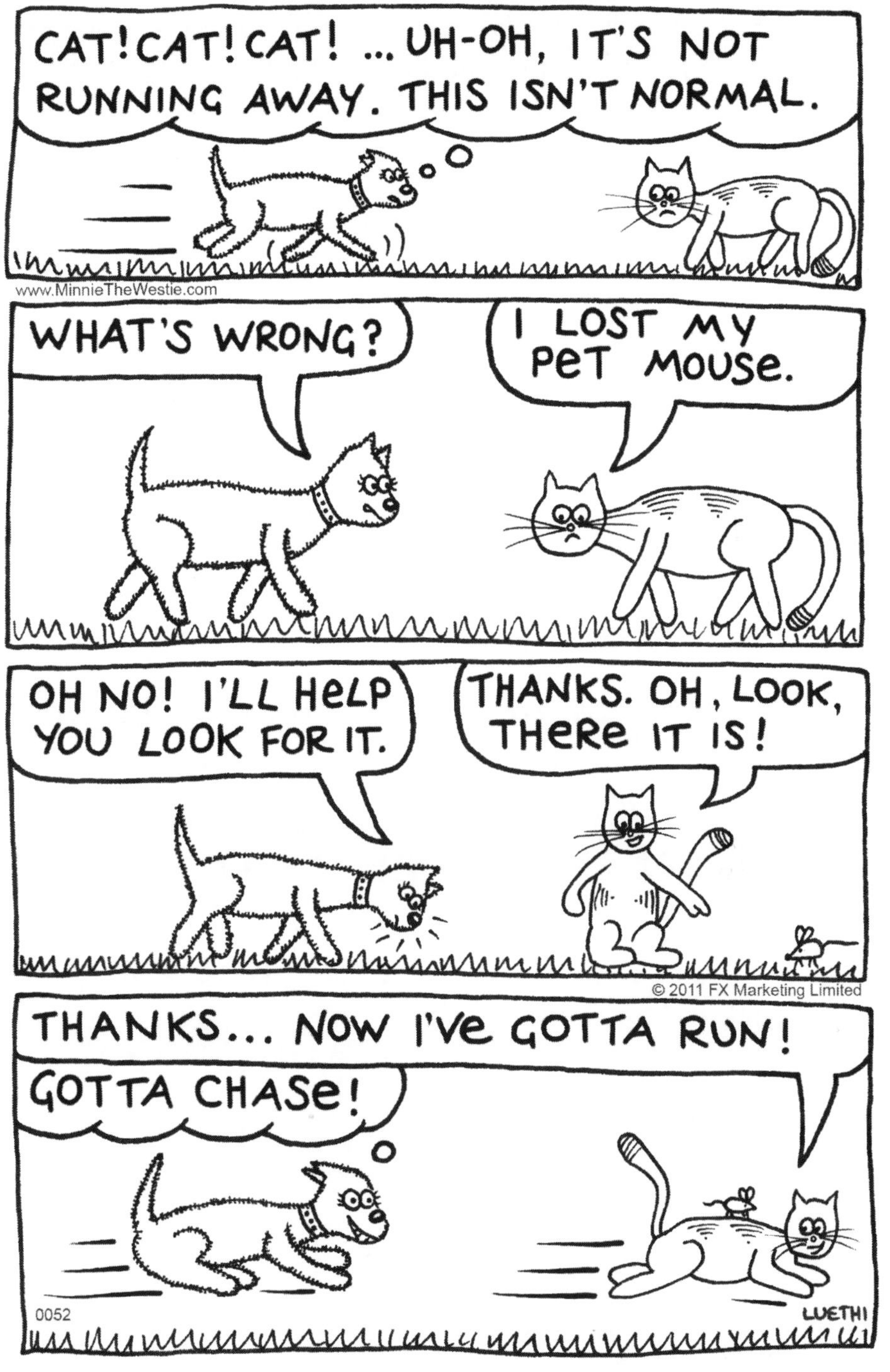
CAT! CAT! CAT! ... UH-OH, IT'S NOT RUNNING AWAY. THIS ISN'T NORMAL.
www.MinnieTheWestie.com
WHAT'S WRONG?
I LOST MY PET MOUSE.
OH NO! I'LL HELP YOU LOOK FOR IT.
THANKS. OH, LOOK, THERE IT IS!
© 2011 FX Marketing Limited
THANKS... NOW I'VE GOTTA RUN!
GOTTA CHASE!
0052
LUETHI

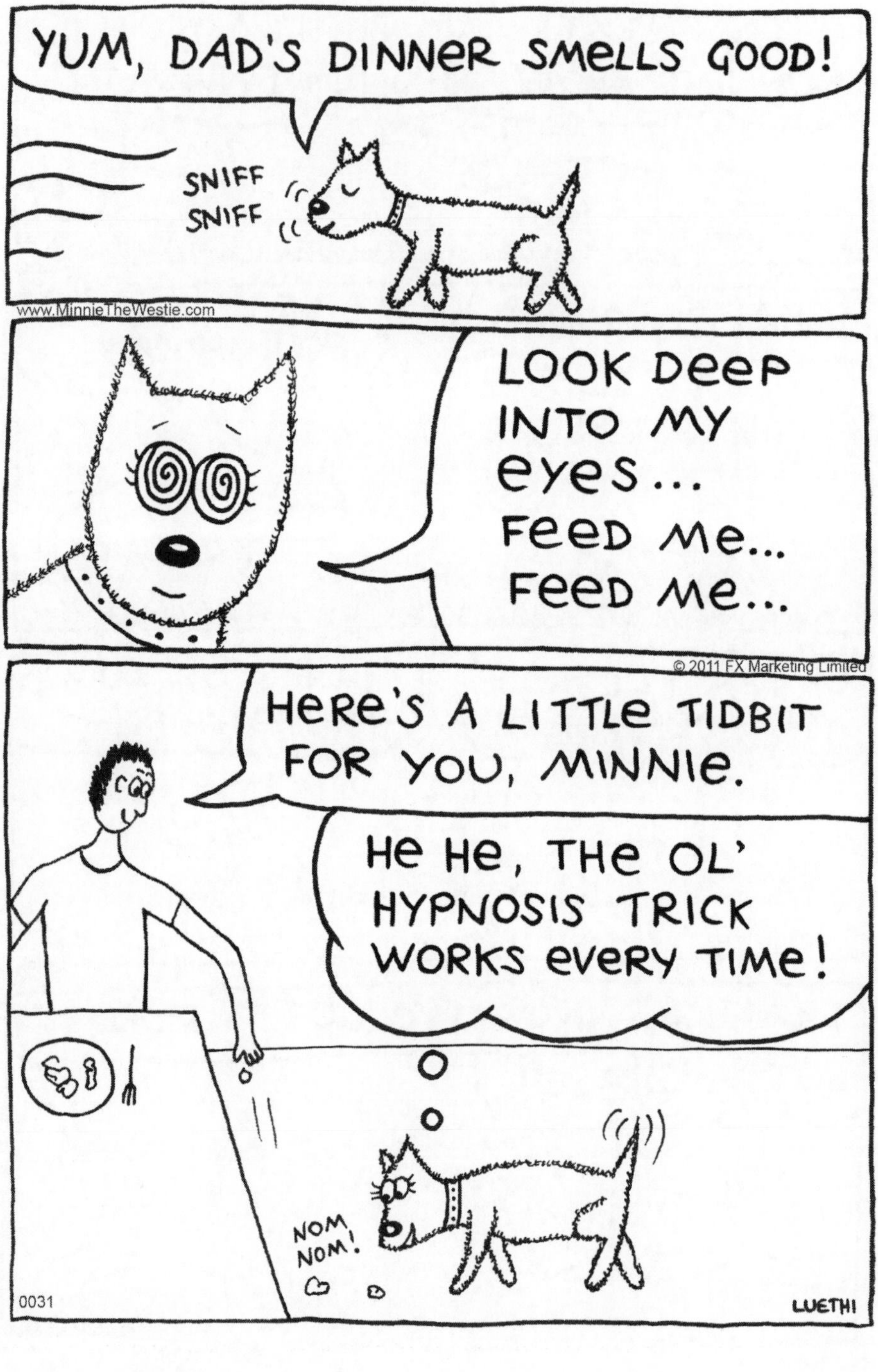
YUM, DAD'S DINNER SMELLS GOOD!
SNIFF SNIFF
www.MinnieTheWestie.com
LOOK DEEP INTO MY EYES... FEED ME... FEED ME...
© 2011 FX Marketing Limited
HERE'S A LITTLE TIDBIT FOR YOU, MINNIE.
HE HE, THE OL' HYPNOSIS TRICK WORKS EVERY TIME!
NOM NOM!
0031
LUETHI

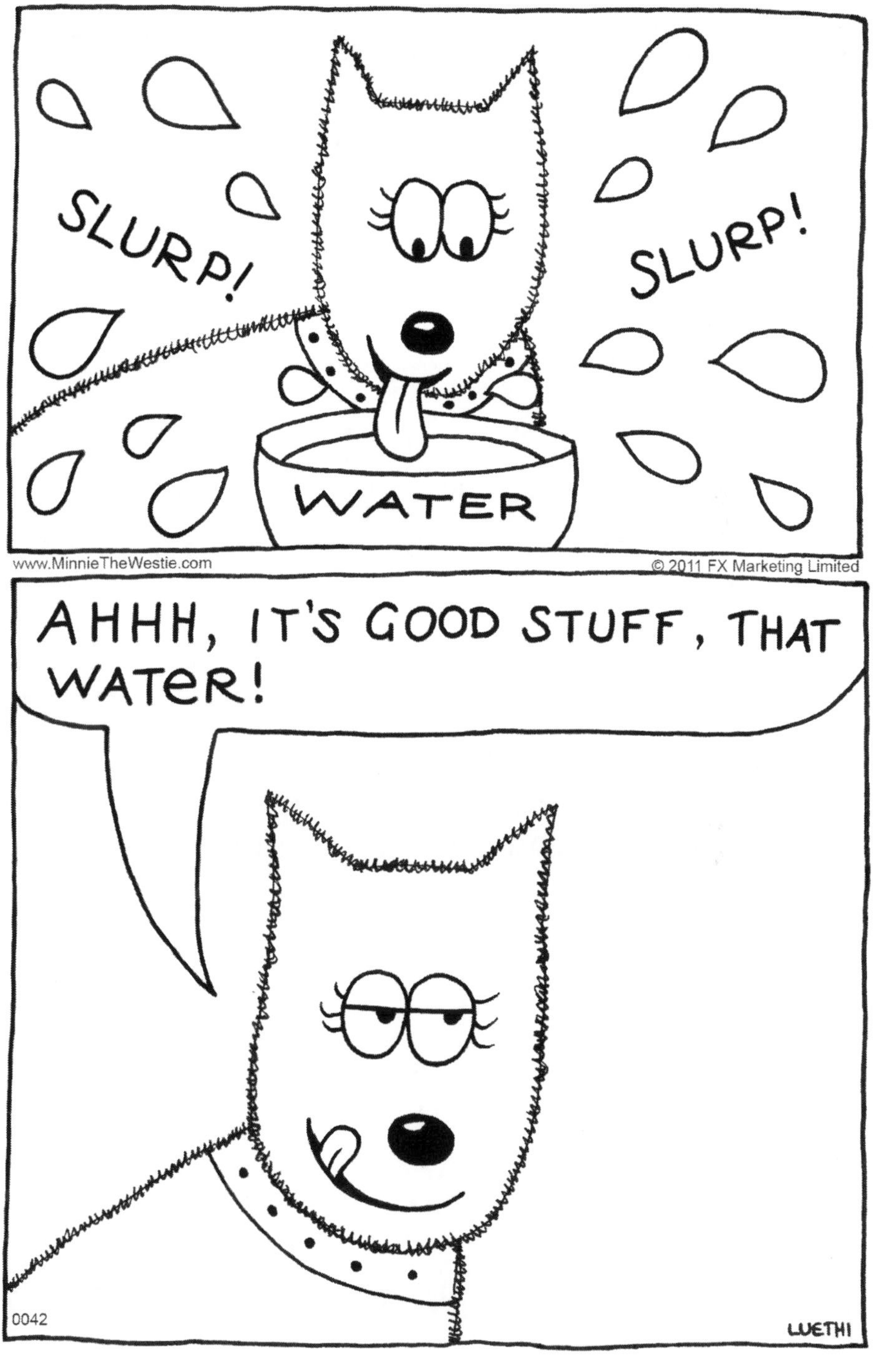
SLURP!
SLURP!
WATER
www.MinnieTheWestie.com
© 2011 FX Marketing Limited
AHHH, IT'S GOOD STUFF, THAT WATER!
0042
LUETHI

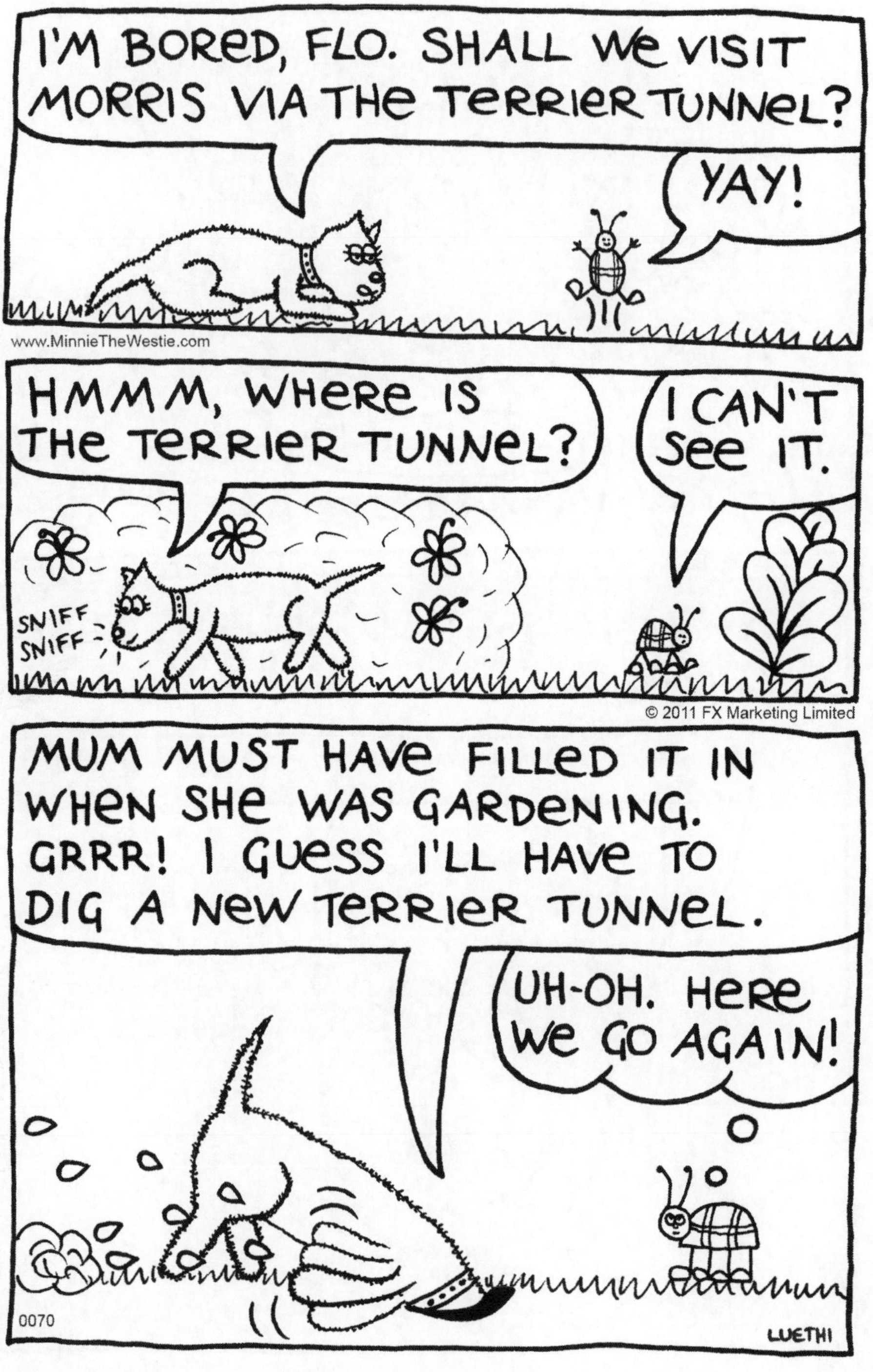
I'M BORED, FLO. SHALL WE VISIT MORRIS VIA THE TERRIER TUNNEL?
YAY!
www.MinnieTheWestie.com
HMMM, WHERE IS THE TERRIER TUNNEL?
I CAN'T SEE IT.
SNIFF SNIFF
© 2011 FX Marketing Limited
MUM MUST HAVE FILLED IT IN WHEN SHE WAS GARDENING. GRRR! I GUESS I'LL HAVE TO DIG A NEW TERRIER TUNNEL.
UH-OH. HERE WE GO AGAIN!
0070
LUETHI

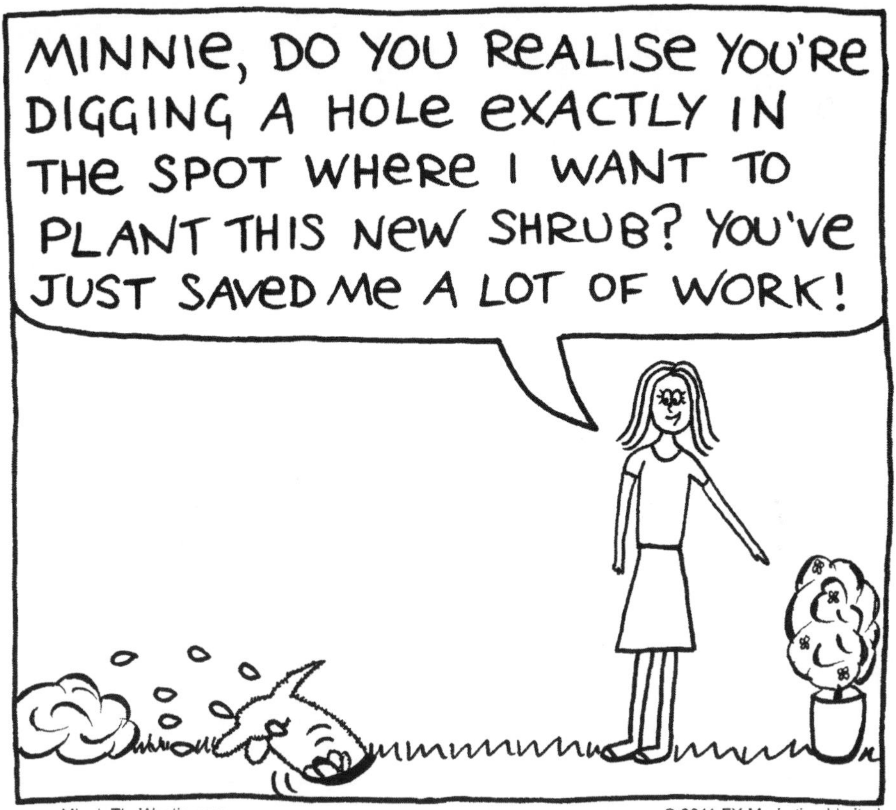
MINNIE, DO YOU REALISE YOU'RE DIGGING A HOLE EXACTLY IN THE SPOT WHERE I WANT TO PLANT THIS NEW SHRUB? YOU'VE JUST SAVED ME A LOT OF WORK!

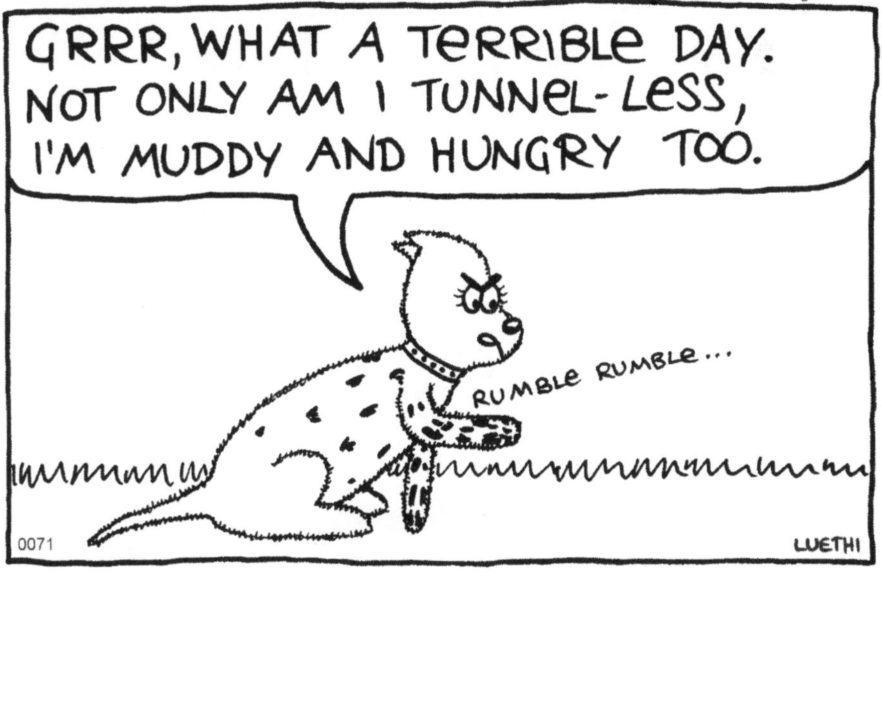
GRRR, WHAT A TERRIBLE DAY. NOT ONLY AM I TUNNEL-LESS, I'M MUDDY AND HUNGRY TOO.
RUMBLE RUMBLE...
0071
LUETHI

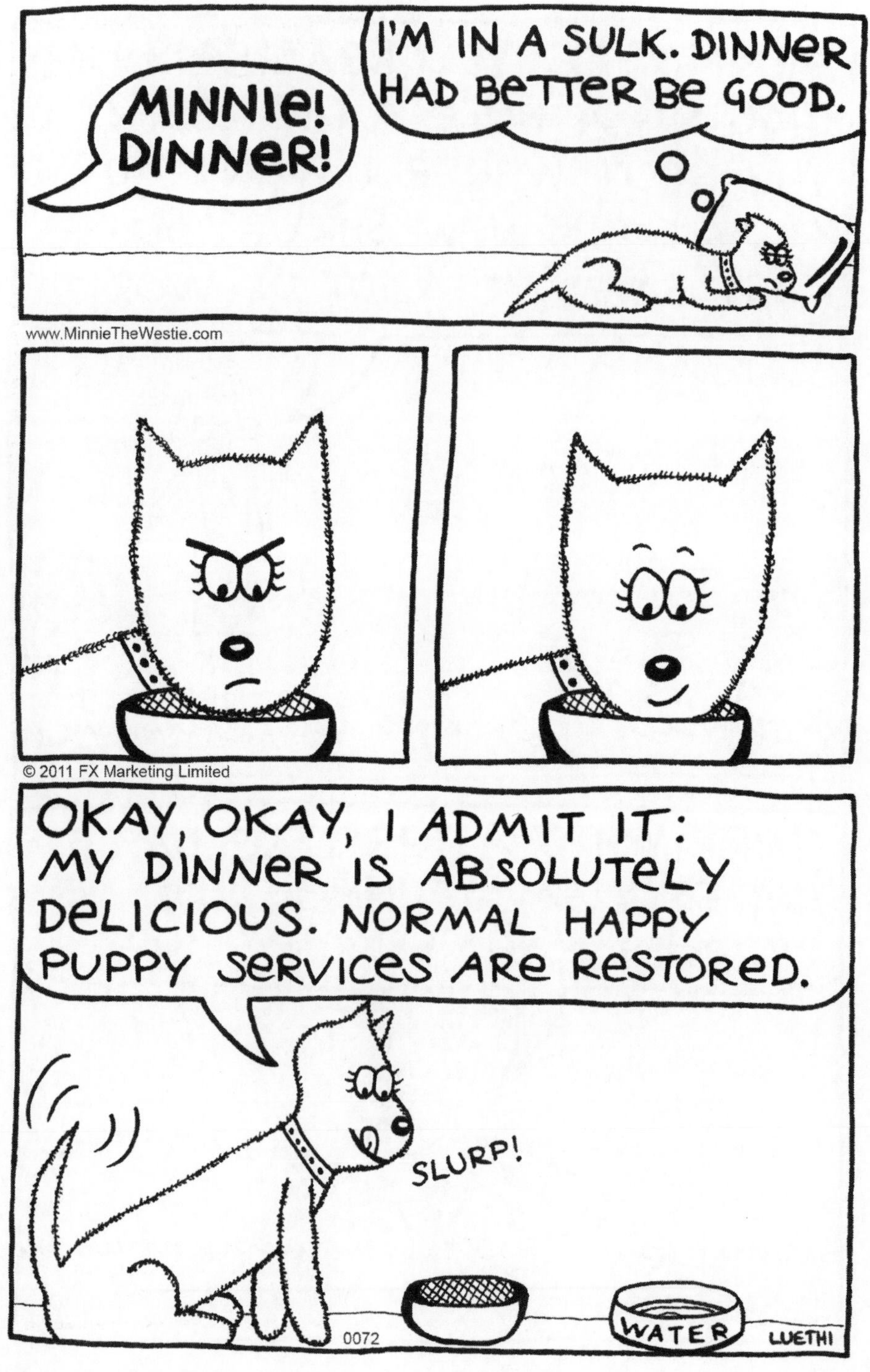
MINNIE! DINNER!
I'M IN A SULK. DINNER HAD BETTER BE GOOD.
www.MinnieTheWestie.com
© 2011 FX Marketing Limited
OKAY, OKAY, I ADMIT IT: MY DINNER IS ABSOLUTELY DELICIOUS. NORMAL HAPPY PUPPY SERVICES ARE RESTORED.
SLURP!
WATER
0072
LUETHI

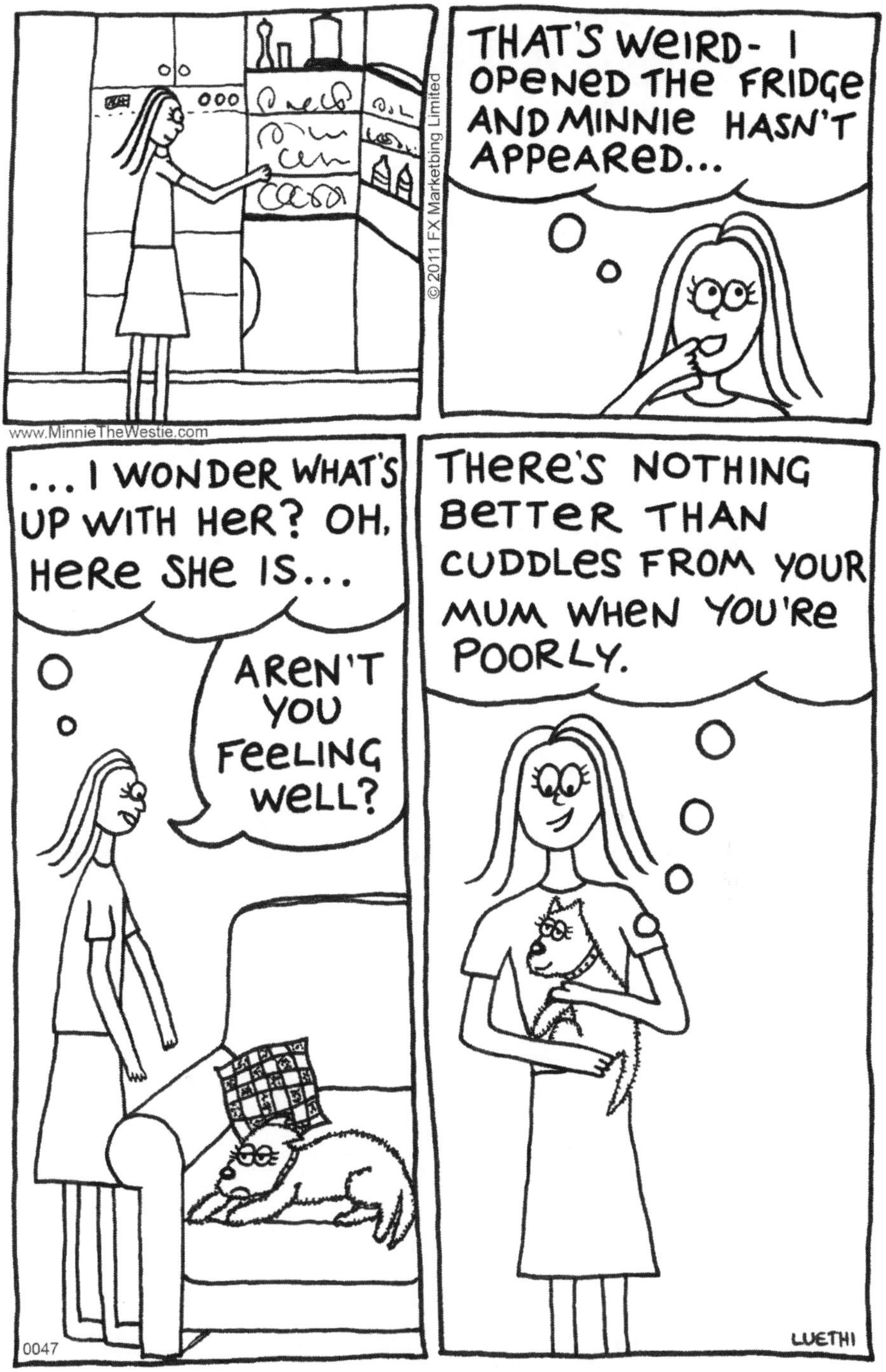
THAT'S WEIRD- I OPENED THE FRIDGE AND MINNIE HASN'T APPEARED...
... I WONDER WHAT'S UP WITH HER? OH, HERE SHE IS...
AREN'T YOU FEELING WELL?
THERE'S NOTHING BETTER THAN CUDDLES FROM YOUR MUM WHEN YOU'RE POORLY.
LUETHI
0047

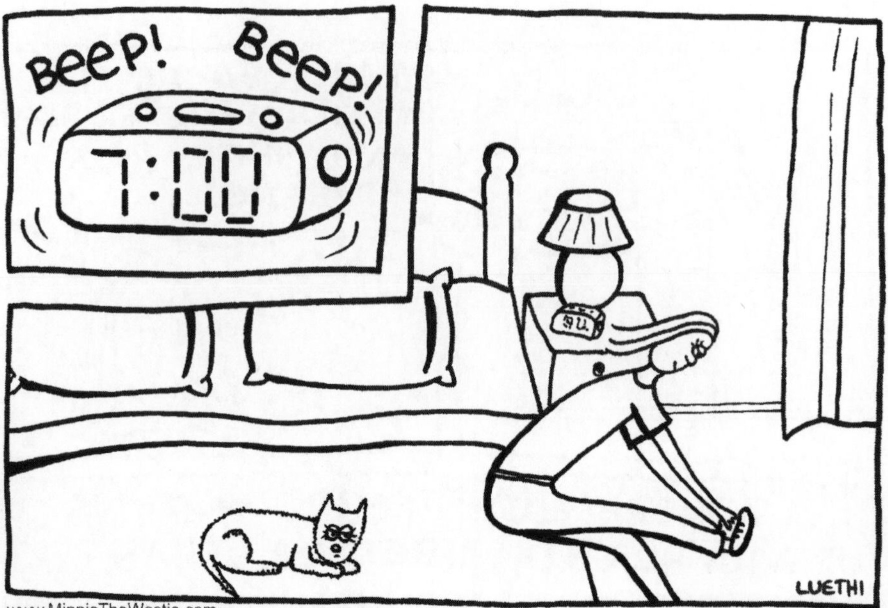
BEEP! BEEP!
7:00
LUETHI

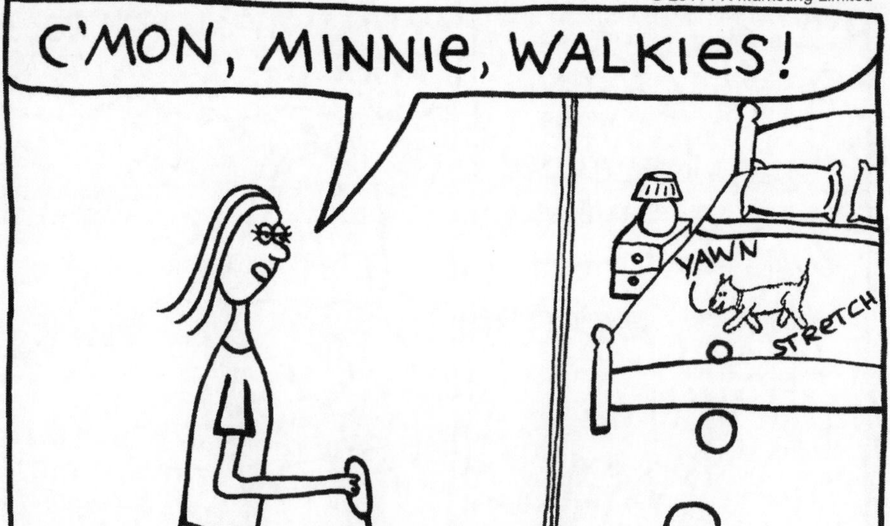
C'MON, MINNIE, WALKIES!
YAWN
STRETCH
0073
COMING! NO POINT GETTING OUT OF BED ANY SOONER THAN ABSOLUTELY NECESSARY!

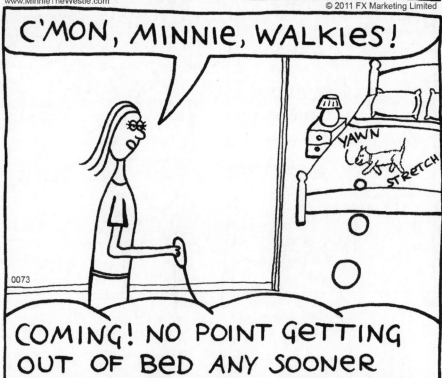

UGH, NEED COFFEE!
I KNOW HOW SHE FEELS; I WISH DOGS COULD DRINK COFFEE.
0046
LUETHI

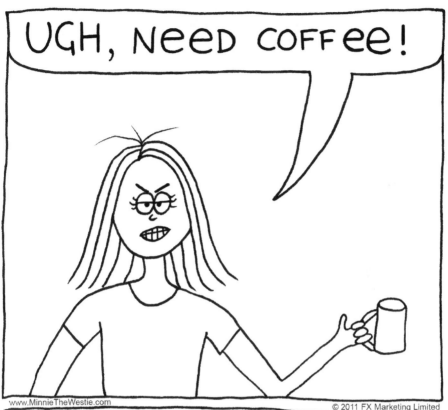

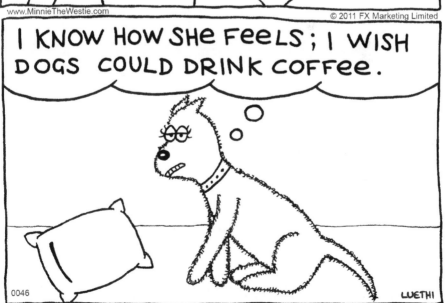

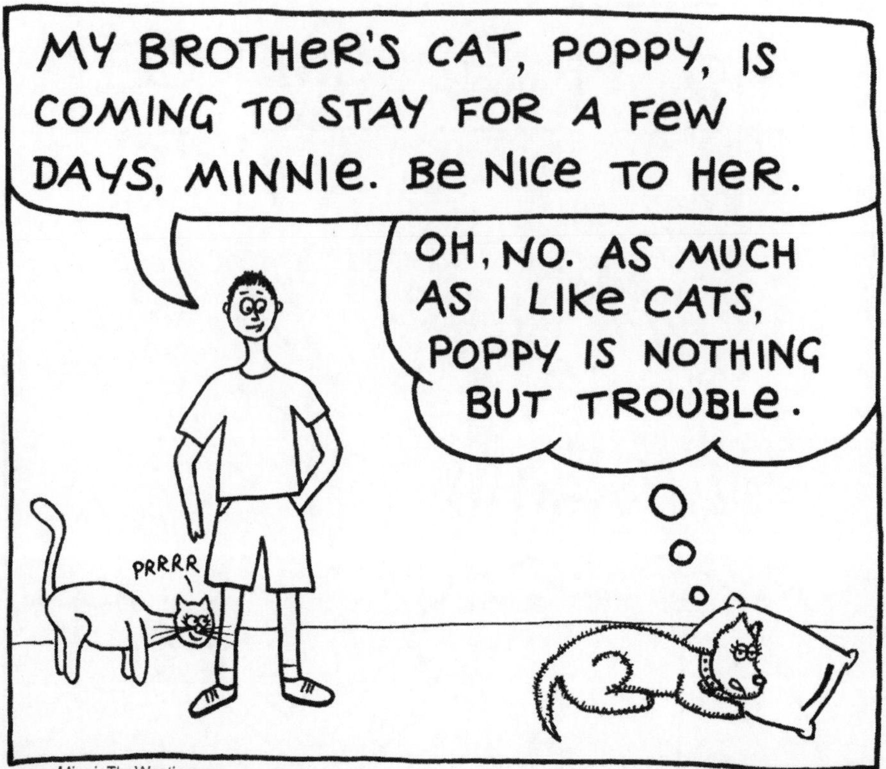
MY BROTHER'S CAT, POPPY, IS COMING TO STAY FOR A FEW DAYS, MINNIE. BE NICE TO HER.
OH, NO. AS MUCH AS I LIKE CATS, POPPY IS NOTHING BUT TROUBLE.
PRRRR

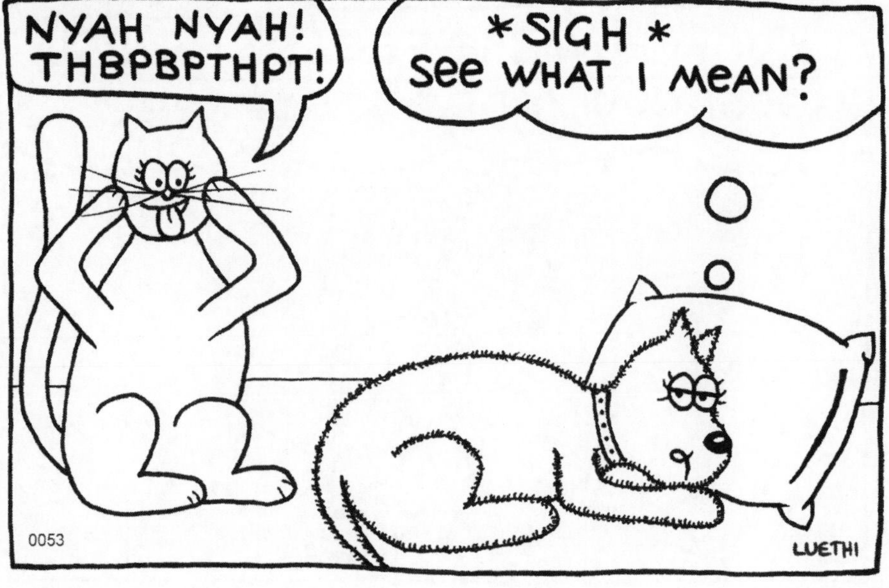
NYAH NYAH! THBPBPTHPT!
SIGH SEE WHAT I MEAN?
0053
LUETHI

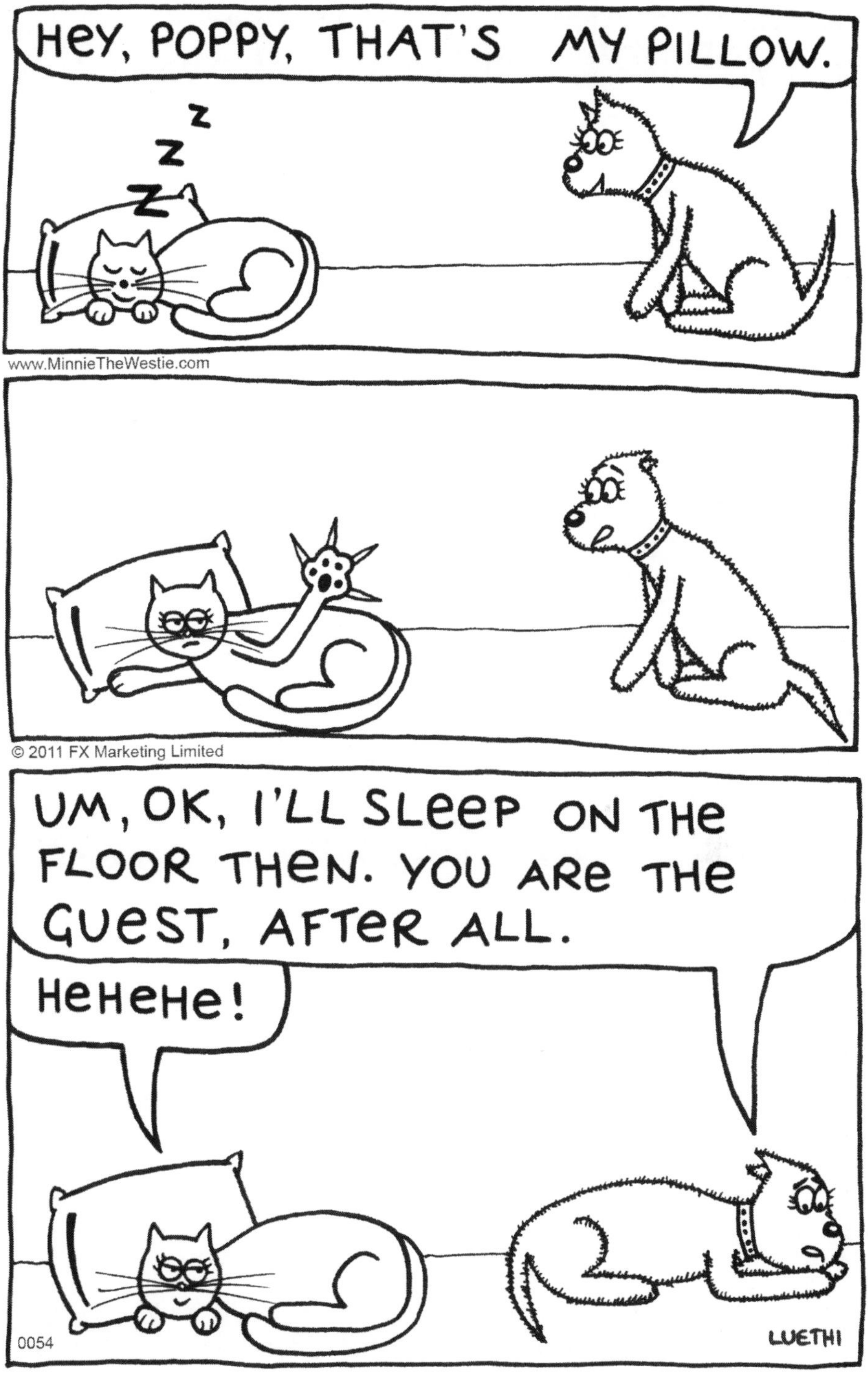
HEY, POPPY, THAT'S MY PILLOW.
Z Z Z
UM, OK, I'LL SLEEP ON THE FLOOR THEN. YOU ARE THE GUEST, AFTER ALL.
HEHEHE!
0054
LUETHI

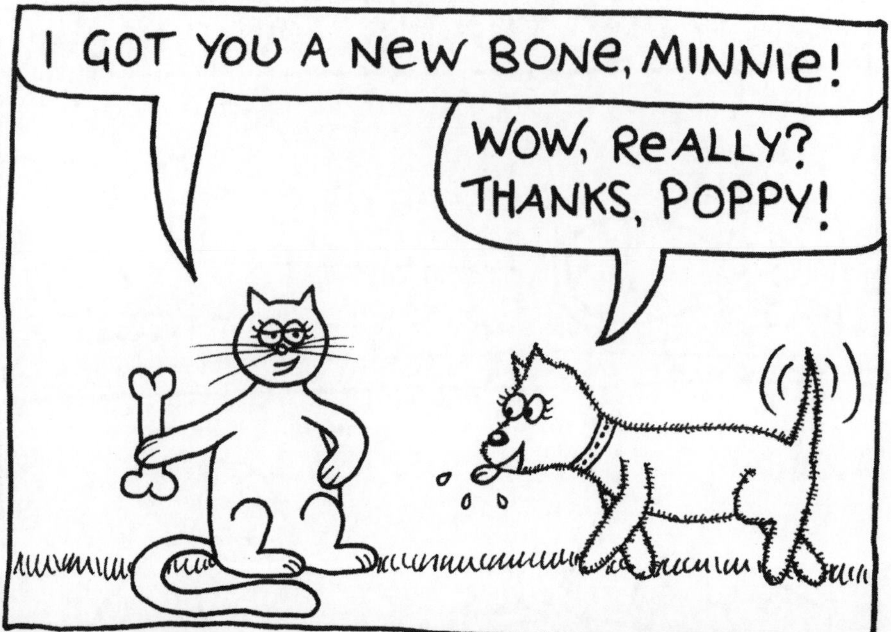
I GOT YOU A NEW BONE, MINNIE!
WOW, REALLY? THANKS, POPPY!

www.MinnieTheWestie.com

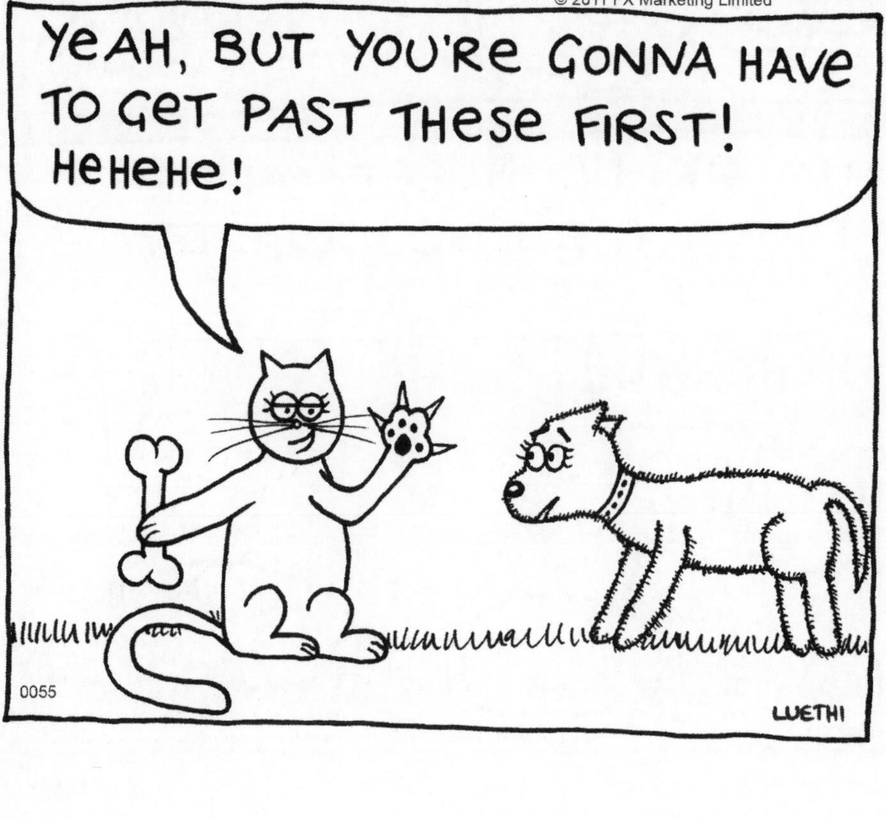
YEAH, BUT YOU'RE GONNA HAVE TO GET PAST THESE FIRST! HEHEHE!
0055
LUETHI

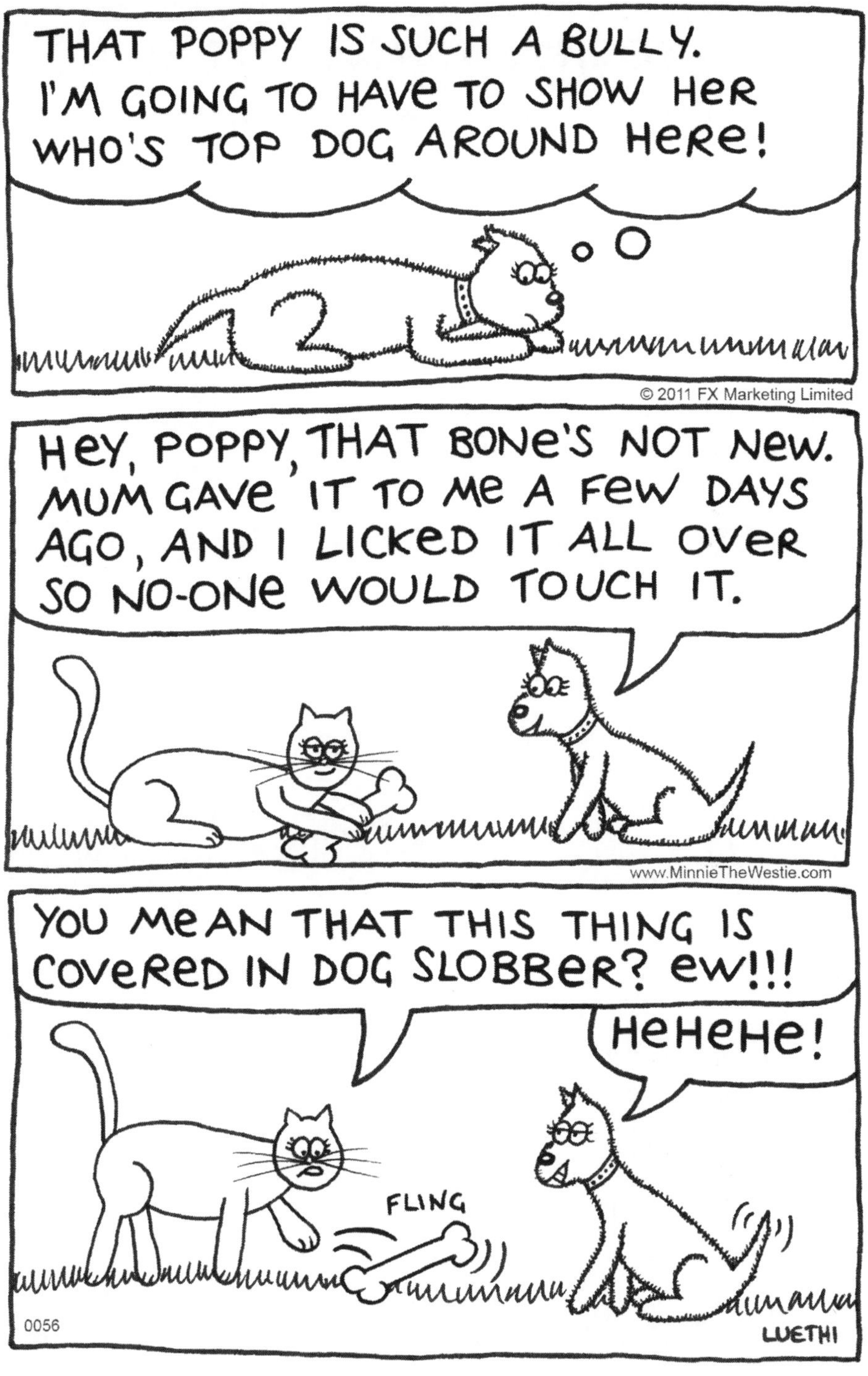
THAT POPPY IS SUCH A BULLY. I'M GOING TO HAVE TO SHOW HER WHO'S TOP DOG AROUND HERE!
HEY, POPPY, THAT BONE'S NOT NEW. MUM GAVE IT TO ME A FEW DAYS AGO, AND I LICKED IT ALL OVER SO NO-ONE WOULD TOUCH IT.
YOU MEAN THAT THIS THING IS COVERED IN DOG SLOBBER? EW!!!
HEHEHE!
FLING
0056
LUETHI

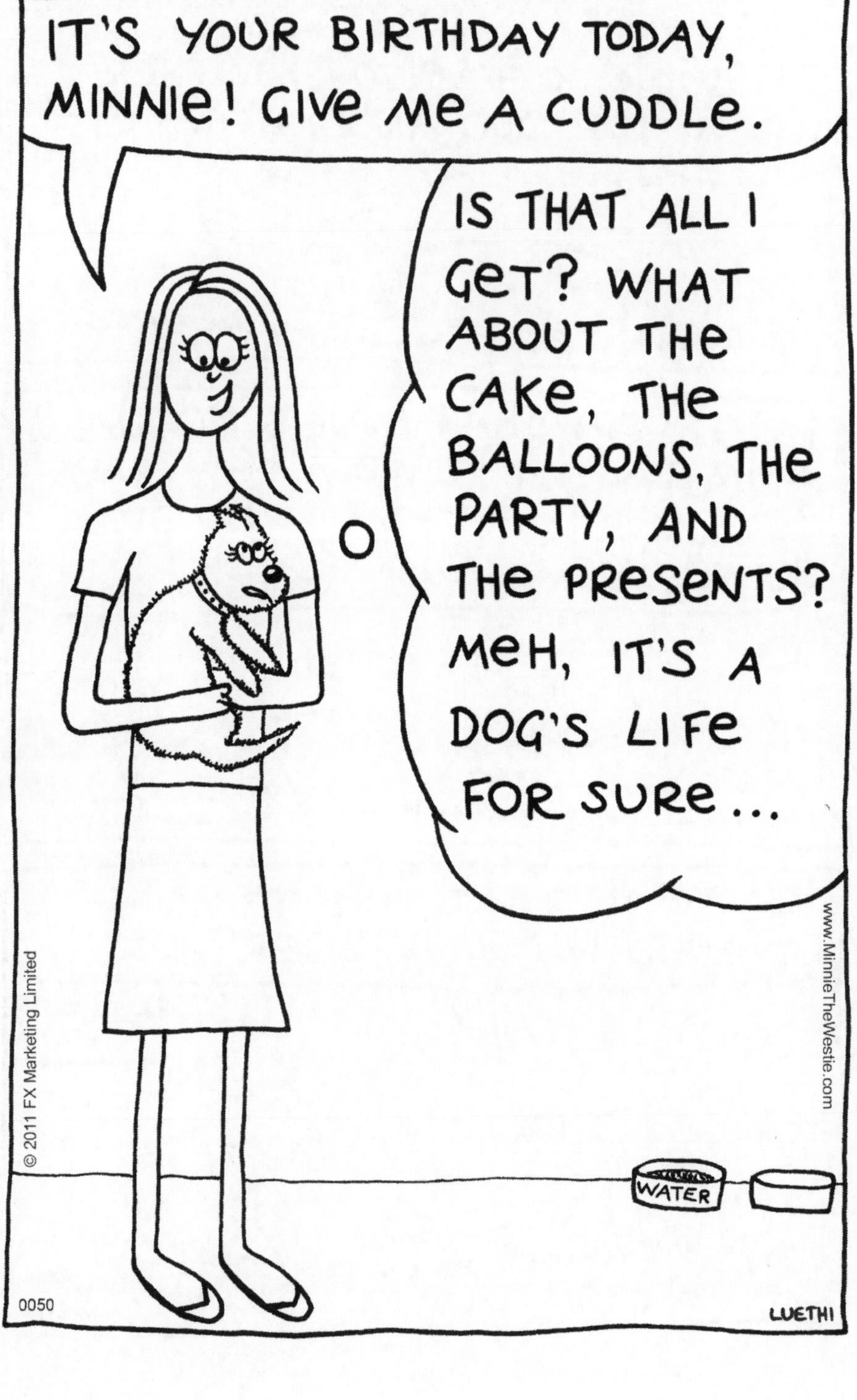
IT'S YOUR BIRTHDAY TODAY, MINNIE! GIVE ME A CUDDLE.
IS THAT ALL I GET? WHAT ABOUT THE CAKE, THE BALLOONS, THE PARTY, AND THE PRESENTS? MEH, IT'S A DOG'S LIFE FOR SURE...
WATER
© 2011 FX Marketing Limited
www.MinnieTheWestie.com
0050
LUETHI

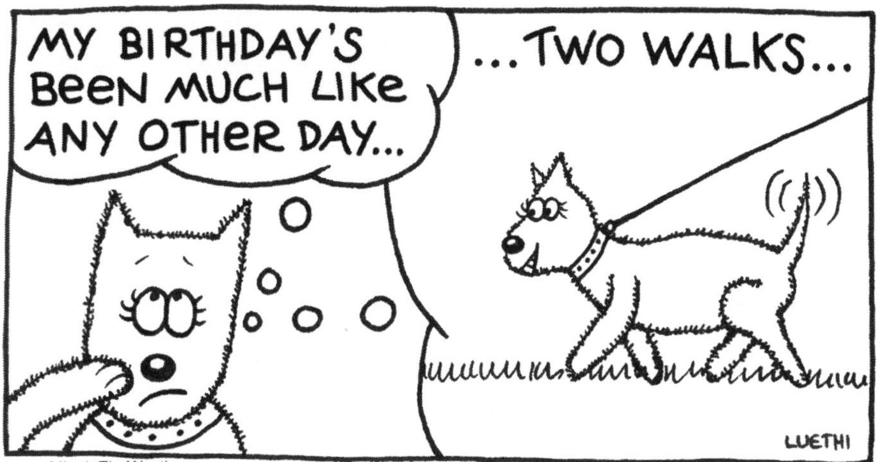
MY BIRTHDAY'S BEEN MUCH LIKE ANY OTHER DAY...
...TWO WALKS...
LUETHI

www.MinnieTheWestie.com

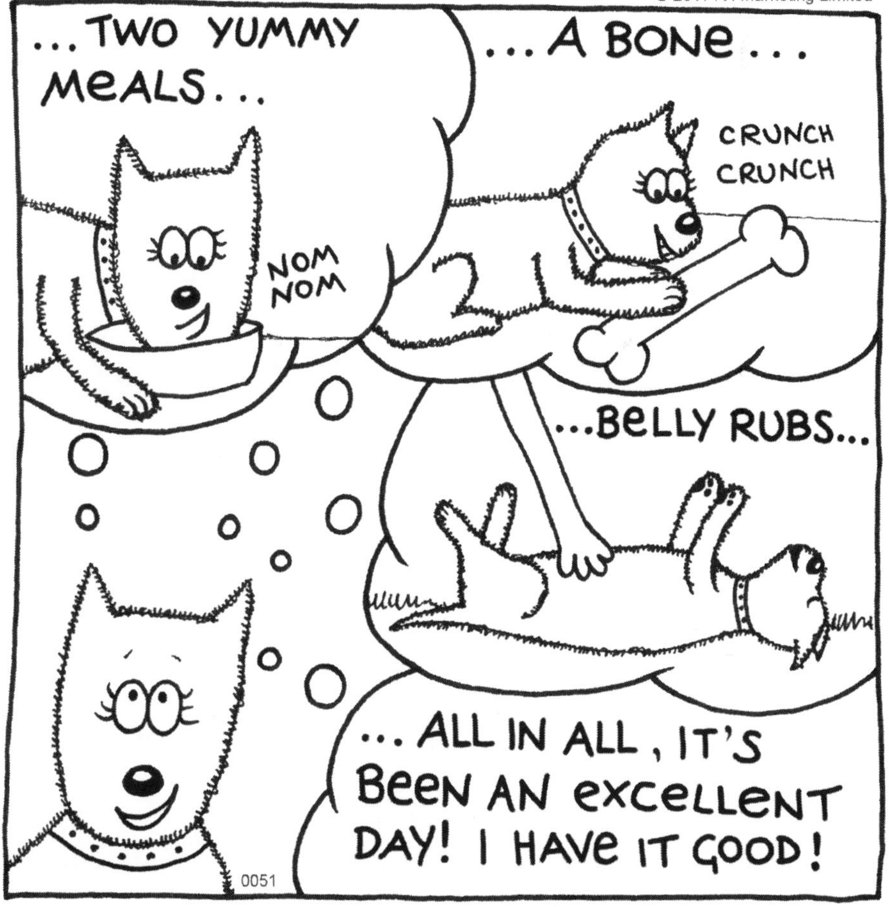
...TWO YUMMY MEALS...
NOM NOM
...A BONE...
CRUNCH CRUNCH
...BELLY RUBS...
...ALL IN ALL, IT'S BEEN AN EXCELLENT DAY! I HAVE IT GOOD!
0051

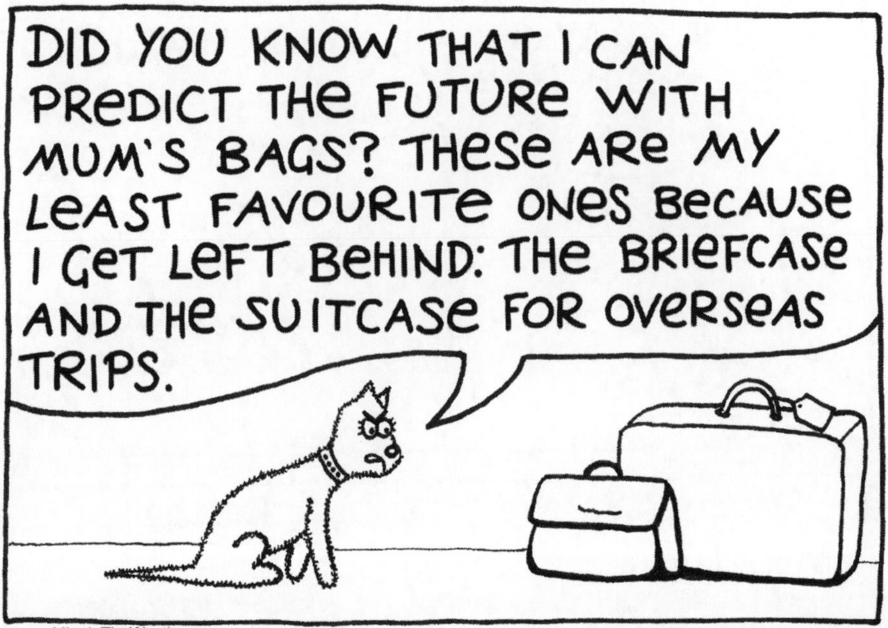
DID YOU KNOW THAT I CAN PREDICT THE FUTURE WITH MUM'S BAGS? THESE ARE MY LEAST FAVOURITE ONES BECAUSE I GET LEFT BEHIND: THE BRIEFCASE AND THE SUITCASE FOR OVERSEAS TRIPS.

www.MinnieTheWestie.com

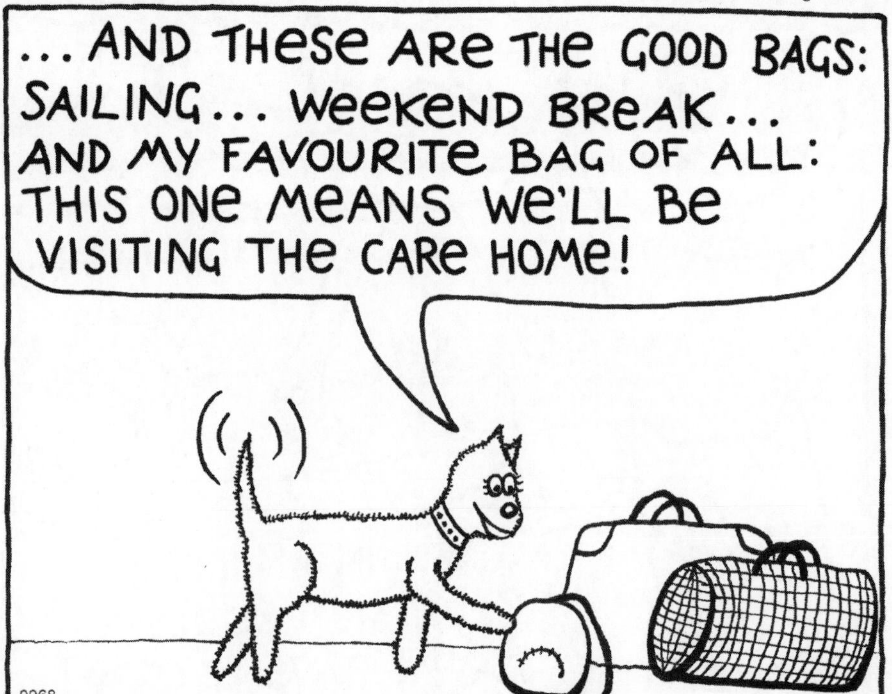
... AND THESE ARE THE GOOD BAGS: SAILING... WEEKEND BREAK... AND MY FAVOURITE BAG OF ALL: THIS ONE MEANS WE'LL BE VISITING THE CARE HOME!
0068
LUETHI

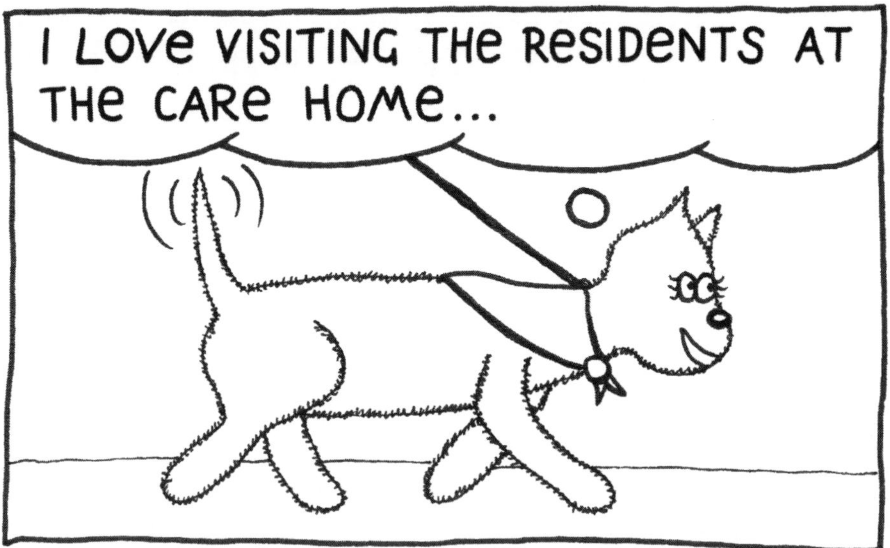
I LOVE VISITING THE RESIDENTS AT THE CARE HOME...

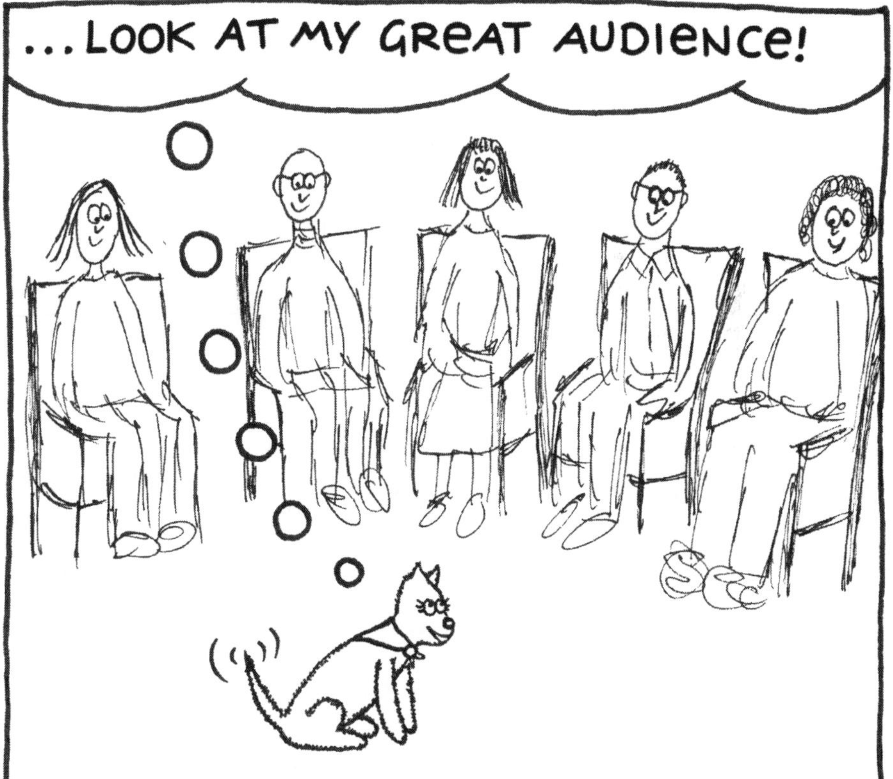
...LOOK AT MY GREAT AUDIENCE!
0076
LUETHI

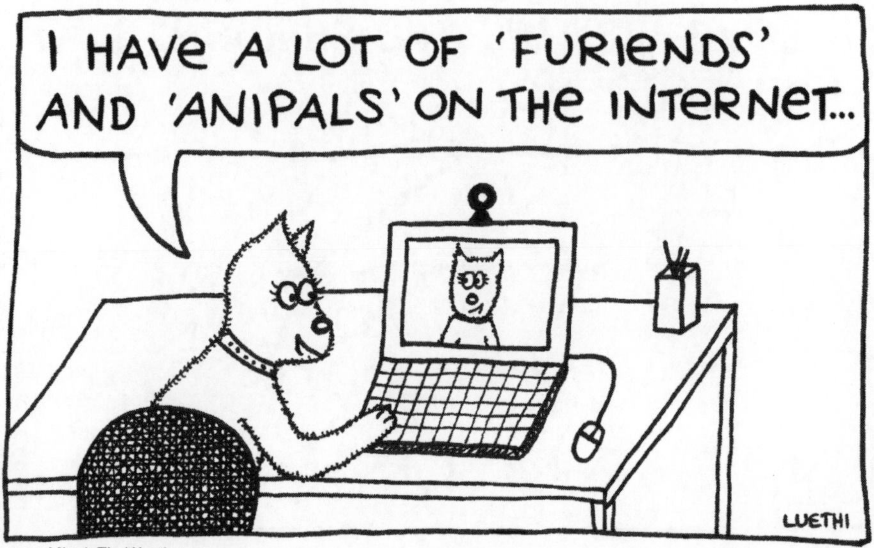
I HAVE A LOT OF 'FURIENDS' AND 'ANIPALS' ON THE INTERNET...
LUETHI

www.MinnieTheWestie.com

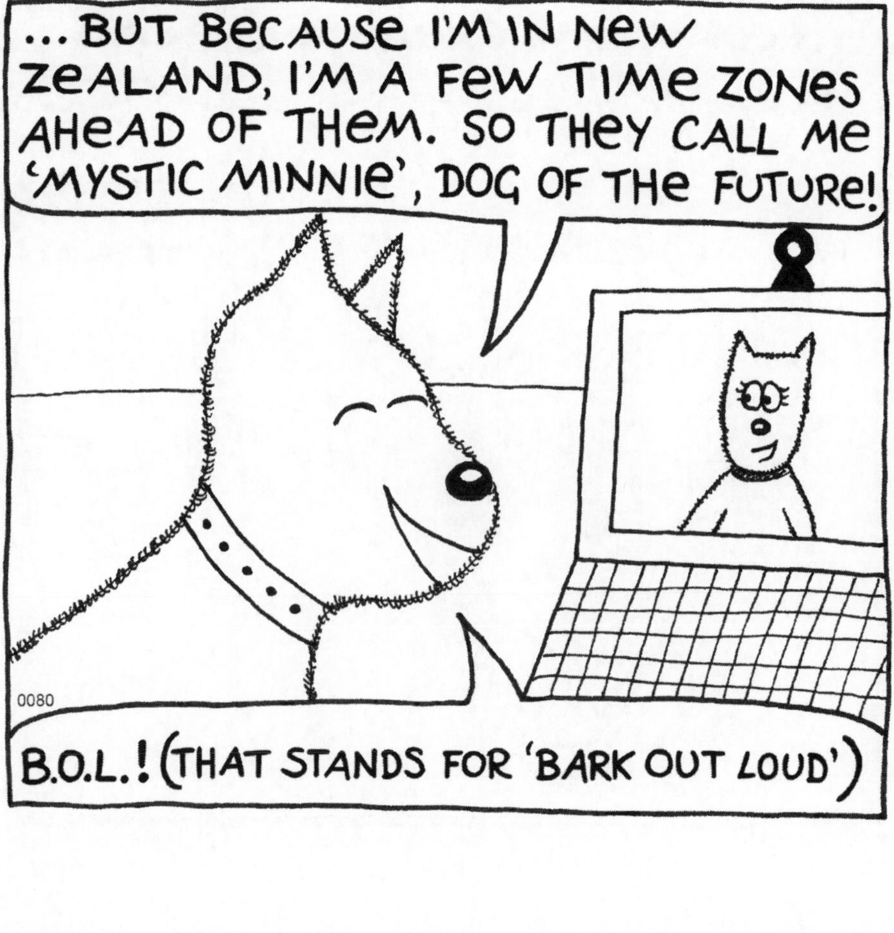
... BUT BECAUSE I'M IN NEW ZEALAND, I'M A FEW TIME ZONES AHEAD OF THEM. SO THEY CALL ME 'MYSTIC MINNIE', DOG OF THE FUTURE!
0080
B.O.L.! (THAT STANDS FOR 'BARK OUT LOUD')

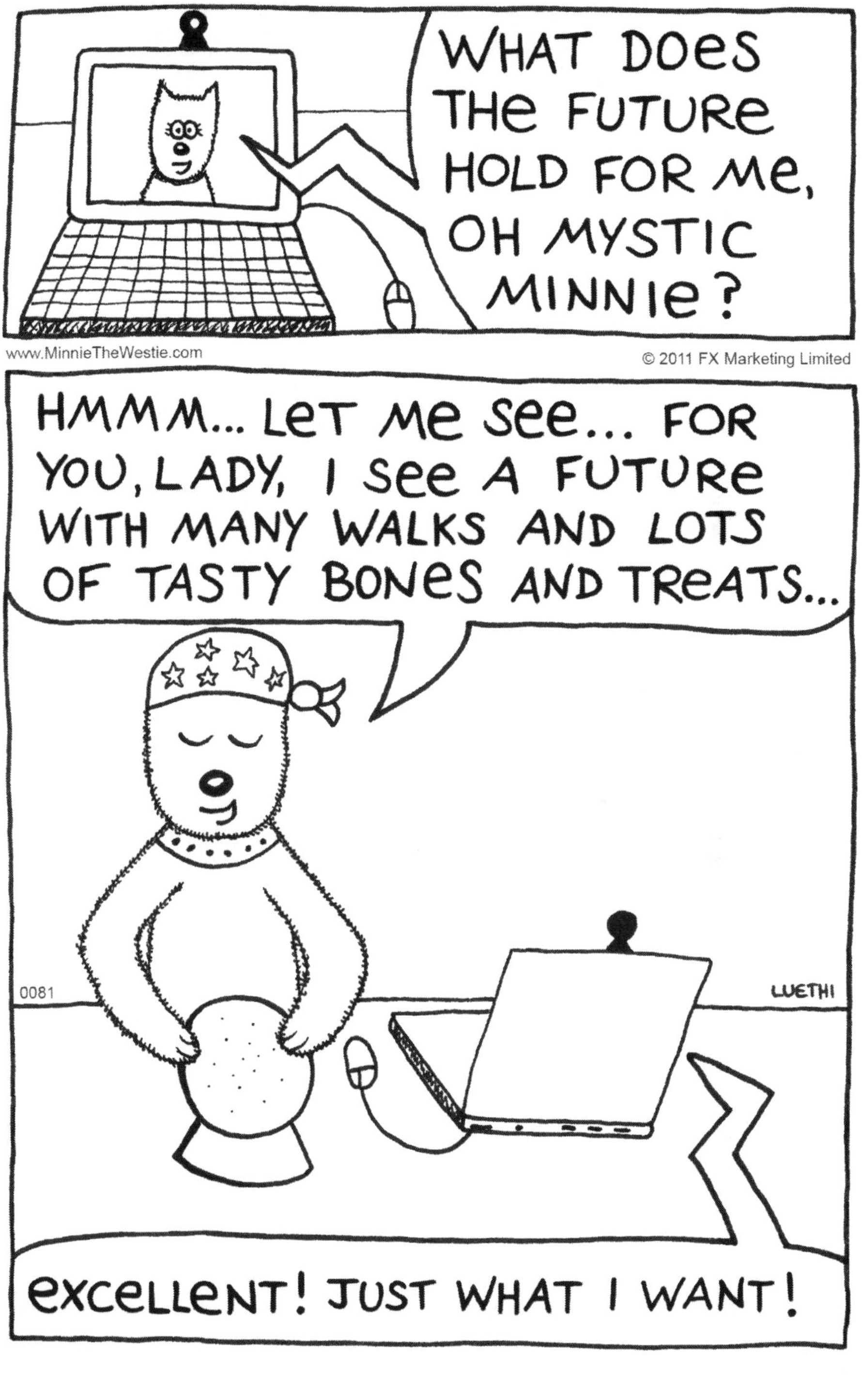
WHAT DOES THE FUTURE HOLD FOR ME, OH MYSTIC MINNIE?
www.MinnieTheWestie.com
© 2011 FX Marketing Limited
HMMM... LET ME SEE... FOR YOU, LADY, I SEE A FUTURE WITH MANY WALKS AND LOTS OF TASTY BONES AND TREATS...
0081
LUETHI
EXCELLENT! JUST WHAT I WANT!

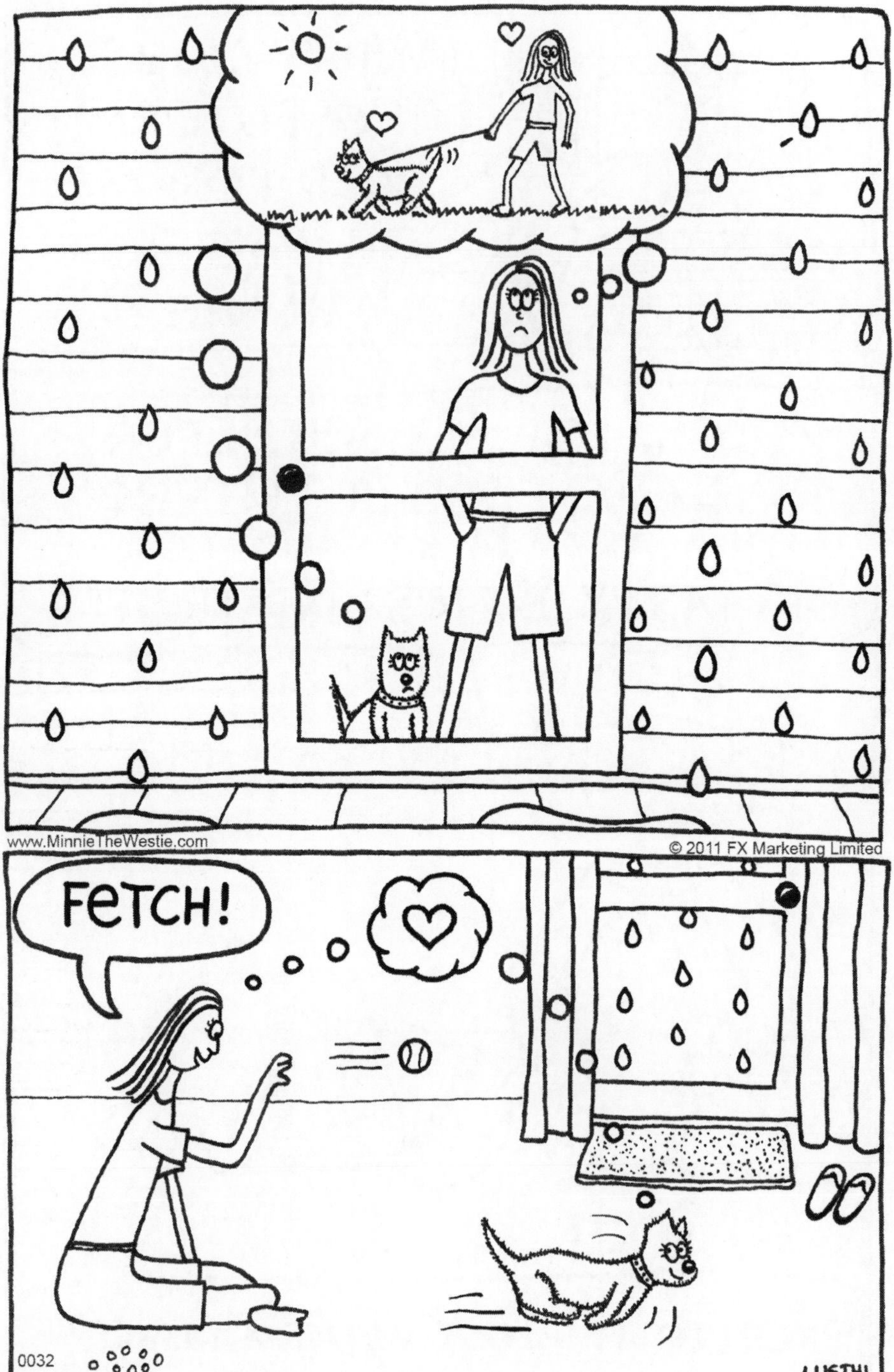
www.MinnieTheWestie.com
© 2011 FX Marketing Limited
FETCH!
0032
LUETHI

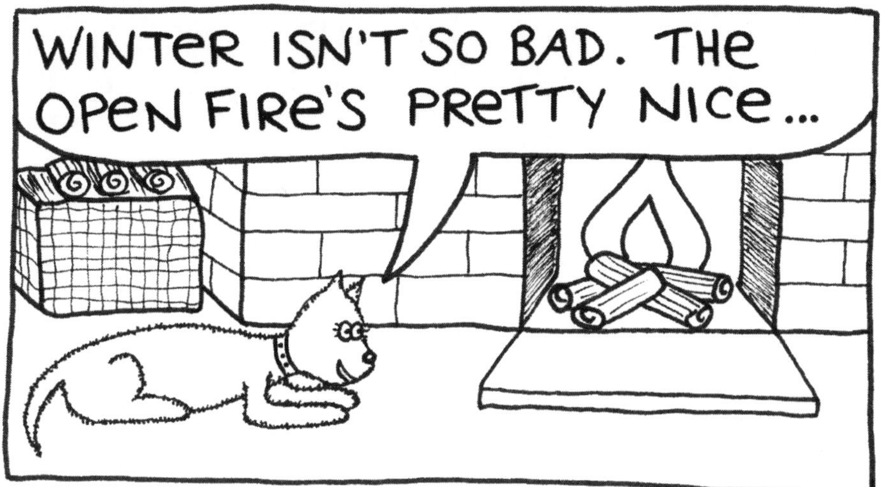
WINTER ISN'T SO BAD. THE OPEN FIRE'S PRETTY NICE...

www.MinnieTheWestie.com

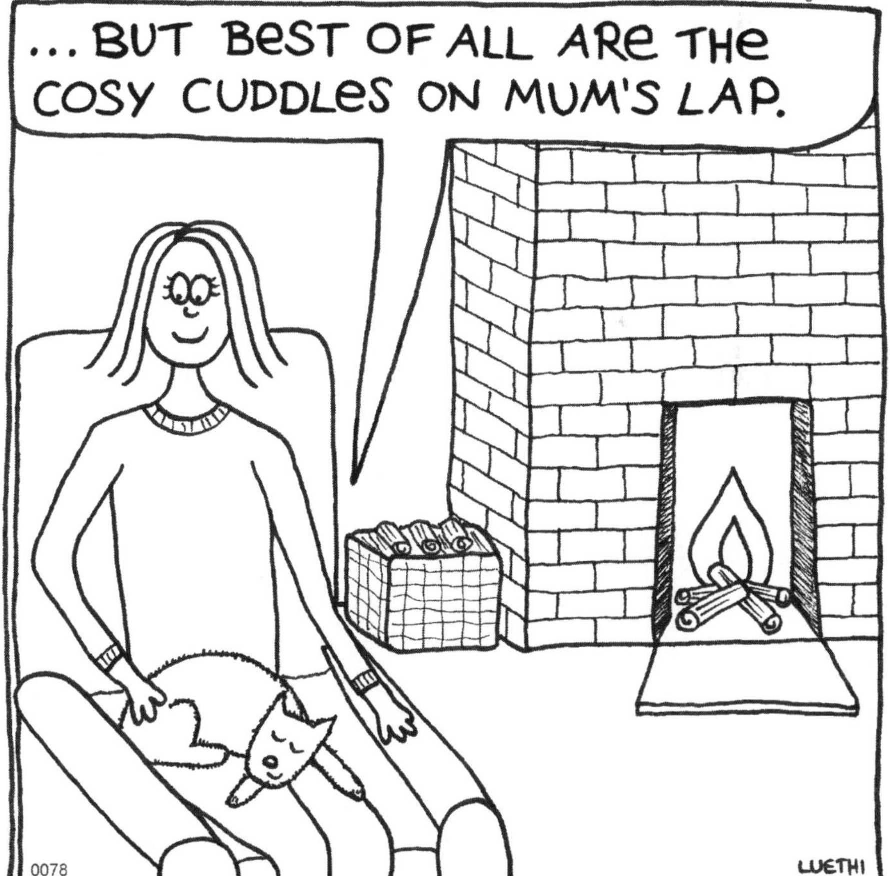
... BUT BEST OF ALL ARE THE COSY CUDDLES ON MUM'S LAP.
0078
LUETHI

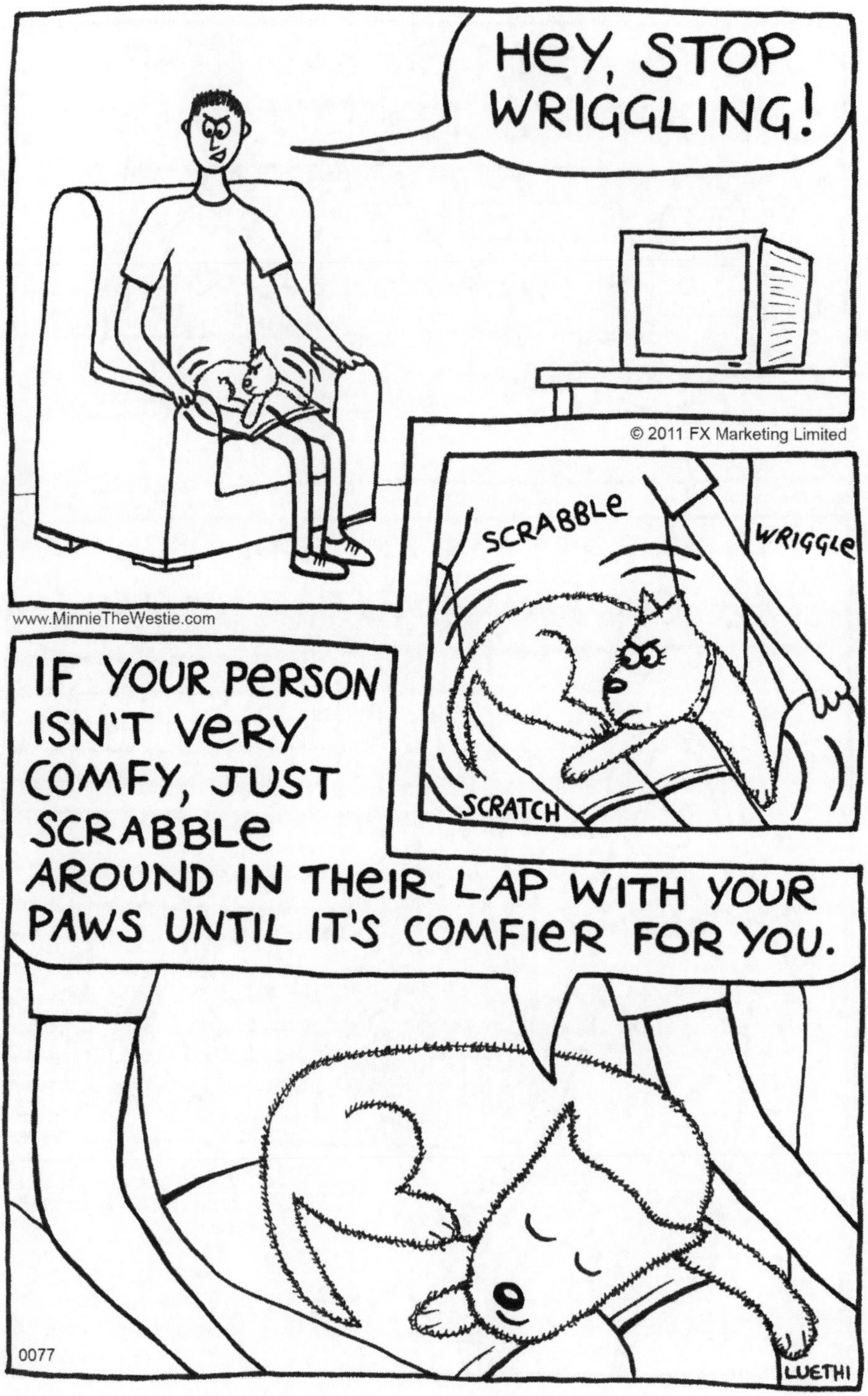

HEY, STOP WRIGGLING!
© 2011 FX Marketing Limited
SCRABBLE
WRIGGLE
SCRATCH
www.MinnieTheWestie.com
IF YOUR PERSON ISN'T VERY COMFY, JUST SCRABBLE AROUND IN THEIR LAP WITH YOUR PAWS UNTIL IT'S COMFIER FOR YOU.
0077
LUETHI

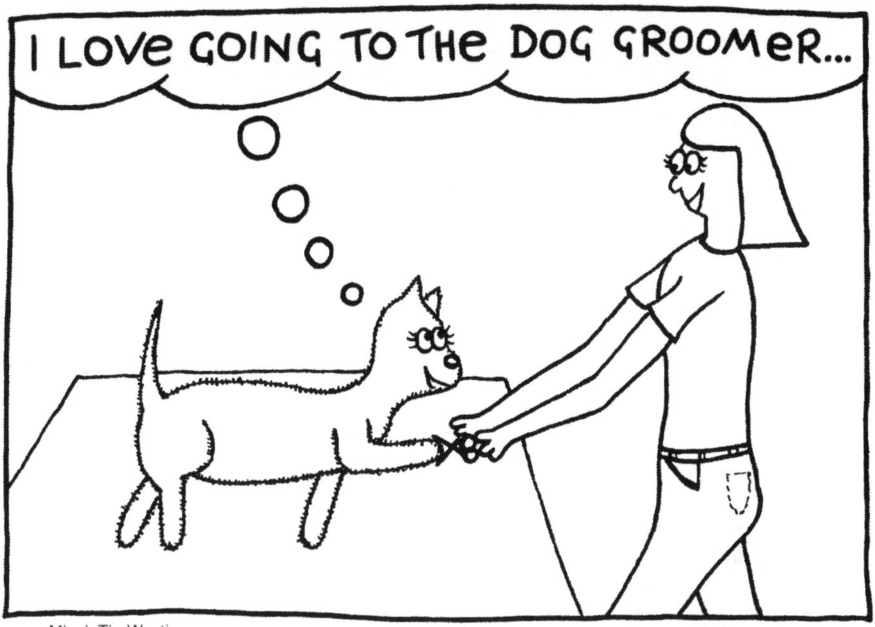
I LOVE GOING TO THE DOG GROOMER...

www.MinnieTheWestie.com

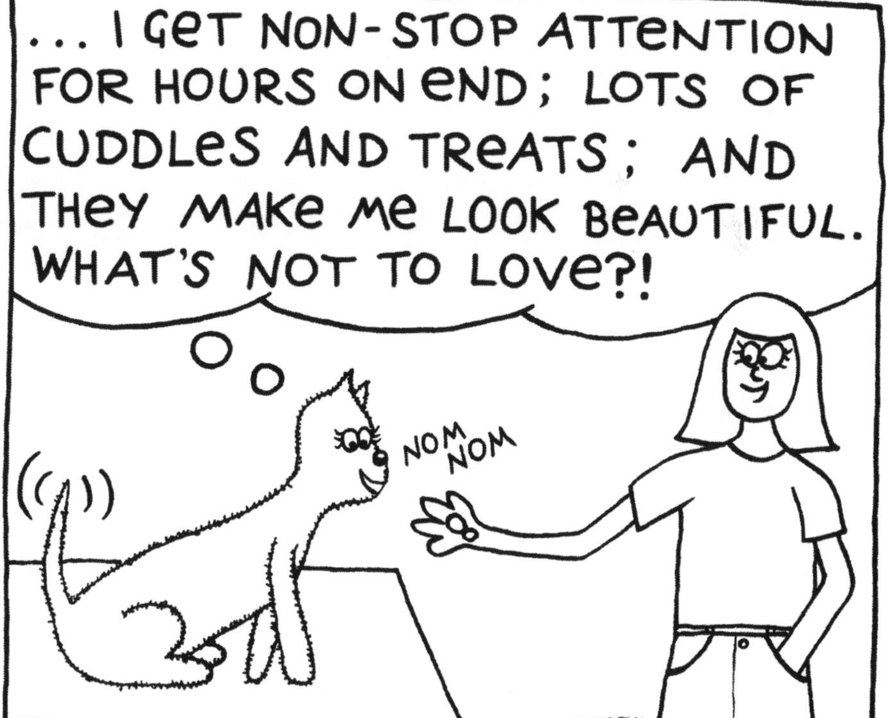
... I GET NON-STOP ATTENTION FOR HOURS ON END; LOTS OF CUDDLES AND TREATS; AND THEY MAKE ME LOOK BEAUTIFUL. WHAT'S NOT TO LOVE?!
NOM NOM
0087
LUETHI

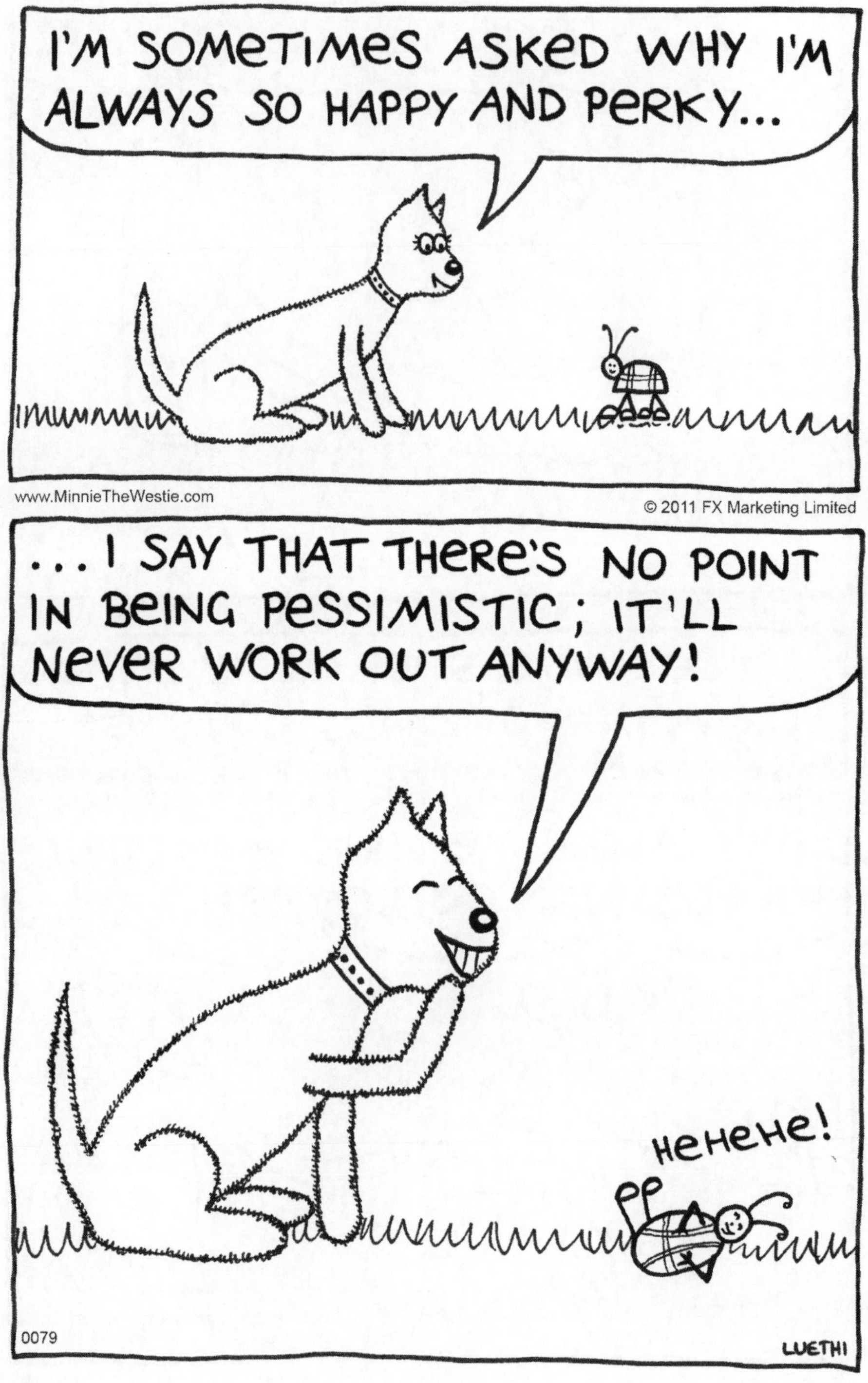
I'M SOMETIMES ASKED WHY I'M ALWAYS SO HAPPY AND PERKY...
www.MinnieTheWestie.com
© 2011 FX Marketing Limited
... I SAY THAT THERE'S NO POINT IN BEING PESSIMISTIC; IT'LL NEVER WORK OUT ANYWAY!
HEHEHE!
0079
LUETHI

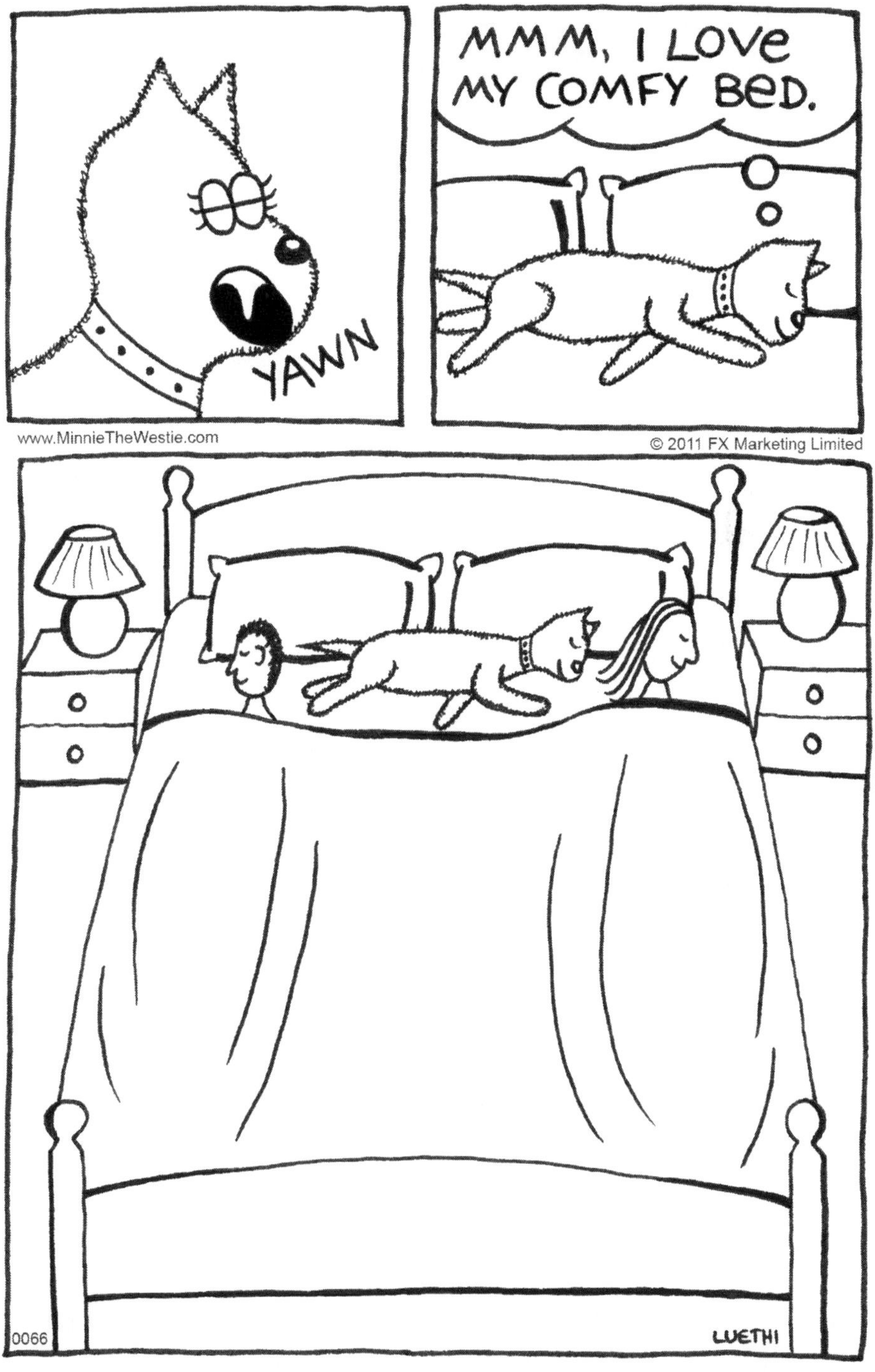
YAWN
MMM, I LOVE MY COMFY BED.
www.MinnieTheWestie.com
© 2011 FX Marketing Limited
0066
LUETHI

Thanks...

Grant ~ thank you for your amazing love and support.

Sean ~ thanks for rekindling my enjoyment of drawing.

Minnie ~ my Bestie Westie, you shall receive your thanks with lots of cuddles, walks and tasty tidbits :)

Minnie The Westie is online!

For more cartoons and Minnie's latest news, visit:

www.MinnieTheWestie.com

You can enjoy cartoons via email with Minnie Mail and connect with Minnie via social media.

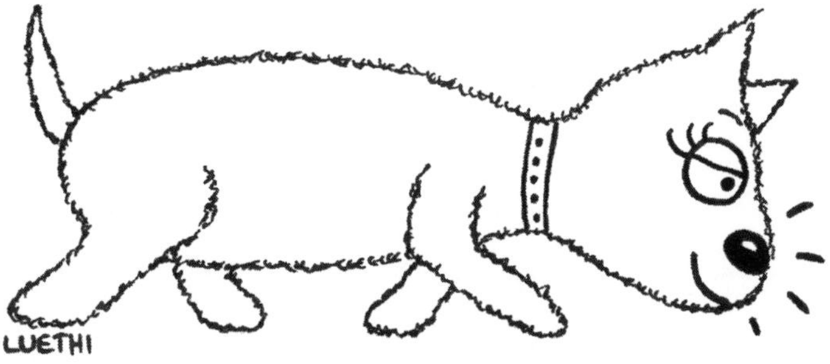
LUETHI

About Minnie and Cornelia Luethi

Cartoon character Minnie The Westie is based on a real life West Highland White Terrier called Minnie. Like her cartoon alter-ego, Minnie lives in Auckland, New Zealand, where she gets to indulge in her favourite hobbies of chicken chomping, bone munching, napping, walking, sailing and cuddling.

Cornelia Luethi is Minnie's Food and Beverage Manager. When Cornelia's not doing that (or drawing cartoons) she runs a marketing consulting business and writes marketing books.

Photo: Minnie and Cornelia on a windy day on Piha Beach, West Auckland. Minnie was a 7 month old puppy at that time and was exhausted after a huge, crazy run on the beach! Happy days :)

Printed in Great Britain
by Amazon.co.uk, Ltd.,
Marston Gate.